Enjoy it
J Hurcomb
13/03/21

ROCKIN' ON THE RIDEAU

OTTAWA'S GOLDEN AGE OF ROCK AND ROLL

JIM HURCOMB

◆ FriesenPress

Suite 300 - 990 Fort St
Victoria, BC, V8V 3K2
Canada

www.friesenpress.com

Copyright © 2021 by Jim Hurcomb
First Edition — 2021

All rights reserved.

No part of this publication may be reproduced in any form, or by any means, electronic or mechanical, including photocopying, recording, or any information browsing, storage, or retrieval system, without permission in writing from FriesenPress.

ISBN
978-1-5255-9335-2 (Hardcover)
978-1-5255-9334-5 (Paperback)
978-1-5255-9336-9 (eBook)

1. Music, Genres & Styles, Rock

Distributed to the trade by The Ingram Book Company

CONTENTS

FOREWORD i
ACKNOWLEDGEMENTS iii
THE KING COMES TO TOWN 1
BEFORE ELVIS 8
THE BEAT GOES ON: 1957 – 1963 12
THE HI-TONES 17
THE JIVE ROCKETS 23
HUGHIE SCOTT 26
SANDY GARDINER AND BEATLEMANIA 30
    SOME "IDOL CHATTER" WITH SANDY GARDINER 31
THE ESQUIRES 35
FEBRUARY 9, 1964: LADIES AND GENTLEMEN…THE BEATLES 39
THE ESQUIRES PT. 2 45
THE STACCATOS: THE LONG WAY HOME 54
    THE SWING SET 59
    SHOW ME THE MONEY! 63
    SOME "IDOL CHATTER" WITH LES EMMERSON 68
    THE FIVE MAN ELECTRICAL BAND RELEASES "SIGNS" 74
GLUED TO THE SET 77

- THE TOWNSMEN 81
  - THE ANIMALS RIOT: MARCH 1, 1967 86
- DON NORMAN AND THE OTHER FOUR 91
- THE BOSS SOUNDS 97
  - SOME "IDOL CHATTER" WITH GORD ATKINSON 100
  - SOME "IDOL CHATTER" WITH AL "PUSSYCAT" PASCAL 103
- SIR JOHN A. RECORDS 110
- THE 5D 116
  - JULY 16, 1968: THE WHO ROCK THE CIVIC CENTRE 120
- THE EYES OF DAWN 122
  - ONE NIGHT IN THE CAPITAL 125
- THE EASTERN PASSAGE 132
- SCOUNDRELZ AND SKALIWAGS, OH MY! 135
  - GERRY BARBER: THE MAN, THE MYTH THE LEGEND 142
- THEE DEUCES/THE HEART 144
  - SOME "IDOL CHATTER" WITH HARVEY GLATT 147
  - GEORGE HARRISON VISITS OTTAWA (?) 151
- THE CHILDREN AND THE MRQ 155
  - DEDICATED FOLLOWERS OF FASHION 158
- FINAL THOUGHTS 166
  - A FINAL "IDOL CHATTER" WITH DICK COOPER 168
    - THE AUDITORIUM 171
    - THE COLISEUM 173
    - CAPITOL THEATRE 174
    - SET LIST FOR JIMI HENDRIX EXPERIENCE LATE SHOW 175

LE HIBOU (Just scratching the surface)	176
HERE AND THERE	177
OTTAWA CIVIC CENTRE	179
ODDS AND SODS	181
TOP FIVE OTTAWA SINGLES OF THE 1960S (?)	182
LEST WE FORGET	**184**
THE BANDS	184
MANAGERS/PROMOTERS	187
ABOUT JIM HURCOMB	**189**

FOREWORD

In the mid-'60s, Britannia ruled the airwaves!

The British music invasion officially arrived on the shores of North America on February 7, 1964, when The Beatles touched down at John F. Kennedy International Airport in New York City. Two nights later, when the first chords of "All My Loving" rang out on the Sunday night variety program *The Ed Sullivan Show*, 73 million viewers, a record for the time, witnessed rock and roll history.

For the next two years, British bands, some good, some terrible, dominated the record charts in the U.S. and Canada. The Dave Clark Five, The Rolling Stones, the Kinks, Gerry and the Pacemakers, Petula Clark, Billy J. Kramer and the Dakotas, Peter and Gordon, Herman's Hermits and countless others rode in the slipstream of the Fab Four and sold in the millions. They also helped rock and roll recover from a disastrous period in popular music when the charts were ruled by bland vocal groups featuring cute boy singers with white teeth, sweaters and nice hair (usually named "Bobby" something) and girl singers in frilly dresses, yearning for love.

The Beatles rescued us from this pop music purgatory. Through 1964 and much of '65, it was all about being British. Up until Bob Dylan plugged in and single-handedly created folk rock in the summer of '65, only a handful of American artists, like The Beach Boys, The Four Seasons, Roy Orbison, The Righteous Brothers, and Gary Lewis and The Playboys, could compete with the Brit bands for chart space.

Here in Canada, rock and roll was in its infancy, played by kids who had seen The Beatles on TV that night or had begged their parents for a guitar when Elvis hit the scene.

Every week, local music fan Doug McKeen put out a chart called *The Swing Set*. It was a small foldout that was published in the newspaper and distributed for free at local record outlets. *The Swing Set* laid out the Top 30 songs in the nation's capital, based on radio play and sales.

The Top 30 from February 15, 1965, featured the usual suspects: The Rolling Stones, The Dave Clark Five, Herman's Hermits, The Righteous Brothers and the Kinks. The Beatles were near the top again with "I Feel Fine." But the #1 song in Ottawa that week didn't come from a British Invasion group. It didn't come from an up-and-coming American artist. It came from The Townsmen, a group from Ottawa.

While the world was swinging to the British beat, Ottawa was riding a rock and roll wave of its own. About half of the population of Ottawa was under twenty-five, and they had money to spend and time to spend it. This sleepy government town, best known for the Parliament Buildings, stodgy bureaucrats, early closing hours and the 150-year-old Rideau Canal, was rockin' after hours in church basements, high school gyms, rec halls and clubs on both sides of the Ottawa River. A homegrown music explosion was under way. This was, indeed, Ottawa's Golden Age of Rock and Roll.

ACKNOWLEDGEMENTS

This book is mainly about the bands and musicians who "made it," whether internationally, nationally, or just locally. It's about them but is dedicated to those who never "made it," who banged out tunes in the garage with their buddies with visions of Elvis and The Beatles twisting in their heads. The ones who played a few basement gigs for friends and just played for the love of it. And it is dedicated to the girls and boys who never picked up an instrument, but who bought the records, went to the dances, and supported the music scene in Ottawa. The magic could not have happened without them.

Nor could this book have happened without the incredible support and involvement of Ottawa's music community. Special thanks go out to Vern Craig and Les Emmerson of The Staccatos, Gary Comeau, Don Norman, Paul Huot and Brian Lewicki of The Esquires, Frank Morrison of The Townsmen, Brad Campbell of the 5D, Hughie Scott, John Bacho, Doug Orr, Marc Corbin, Ken Lauzon, John Martin and so many other great musicians.

Bob St. George of The Hi-Tones and Jack MacDonald of the Jive Rockets provided some very rare photos from the late 1950s and '60s, and Don Norman, Vern Craig and Gary Comeau were also generous with their private photo collections.

Procuring visual material for a book like this is essential, and it can also be a giant headache securing rights to use photos. Thankfully, John Lund from the City of Ottawa Archives loved the idea and gave me permission to use the legendary Elvis photos and more snapshots of Ottawa in the 1960s. And out of the blue I lucked into the classic shot of young Paul Anka when famed Ottawa photographer Jean-Marc Carisse posted it on Facebook. I contacted him, explained what I was doing, and he immediately gave me his blessing to use the photo.

Special thanks to my "secret weapon," Ken Creighton. Ken heard about *Rockin' on the Rideau* and told me he had some material I might be interested in looking at. It turned out to be a treasure trove of band photos and lists that Ken had compiled when he was working on a similar project years ago. Without Ken's generosity, this book would have been much poorer.

Thanks as well to Dave Sampson and Ian McLeish who have dedicated so much of their time over the years to keep the flame alive when it comes to local music, especially the sounds of the '60s.

Just in case you don't recognize the cherubic young man on the front cover, Richard Patterson was the drummer for the Electrons, The Esquires, Canada Goose and other key bands in our story. We lost Richard way too soon.

I don't know much about the photo that appears at the end of this section. It is just a cool image that captures the times. It made me smile and flash back to my early days in bands. A young musician poses proudly in front on his bands' van, child in arms. Don't know much about "The Plague", but I do know that today the kid, Dan Youngs, sits behind a big desk as Program Director for Ottawa's LIVE88.5. Never hurts to put your boss in a book!

Writing a book takes intense focus and drive to get from "once upon a time" to "happily ever after." Those two qualities don't come to me naturally, so thanks to Diane, Kelly, Emma and Jamie for inspiring me with all they have achieved in their short lives. It's sometimes hard for Dad to keep up.

To those I missed: thank you, thank you, thank you. I hope you enjoy the results.

So, without further ado, "Once upon a time…"

For Those About to Rock...

THE KING COMES TO TOWN

Ottawa fans welcome Elvis

The date was April 3, 1957. That was the day Elvis Presley came to town to play two shows at the old Ottawa Auditorium on the corner of Argyle and O'Connor.

Best known as one of your classic Canadian "hockey barns," the 10,000-person capacity "Aud" was built in 1923 as the home of the Ottawa Senators of the NHL. Over the years, the Aud also featured boxing exhibitions with Joe Louis and Rocky Marciano, tennis matches with Bill Tilden and Bobby Riggs, and appearances by the Red Army Choir, John Philip Sousa and the Harlem Globetrotters. CFRA had its first radio studio in the Aud, and kicked off their broadcasting life in May 1947 with a live concert by Percy Faith and his orchestra. Before the wrecking ball dropped to make room for the YM/YWCA building in 1967, the Aud had also played host to music legends like Buddy Holly, Brenda Lee, Bob Dylan, Frank Sinatra, Ray Charles, The Everly Brothers and The Rolling Stones. But on that cool spring day in 1957, it was "The King" who played the most famous gig in Ottawa music history.

The famed Ottawa Auditorium

Elvis did two shows that day, the first at 5 p.m., the second at 8:30 p.m. Nine thousand delirious fans crammed into the Auditorium clutching their golden tickets, which ranged in price from $2.00 to $3.50.

It was the only time Elvis would tour outside of the United States. His manager, "Colonel" Tom Parker, a character whose picture could have graced a bucket of fried chicken, was actually from Holland, and an illegal immigrant to the States. He was afraid if he left the country he might never get back in, so was quite content to make American dollars for the rest of Elvis' career.

A major step along Elvis' stairway to the stars was the epic performance on *The Ed Sullivan Show* seven months earlier. Just as the next generation would never forget The Beatles on that same show in 1964, when Elvis hit the grainy screen that night, the world stopped and then re-started in a different gear.

About 700 kilometres north of CBS-TV Studio 50 on Broadway, twelve-year-old Don Norman and his sister watched with their parents as the skinny kid from Tupelo ripped through "Don't Be Cruel," "Ready Teddy" and his signature show-stopper, "Hound Dog." Don remembers, "He was so different. We had never seen anything like it."

Up to that point Don had been an accomplished "hairbrush singer," miming to the crooners of the day. But Elvis changed the repertoire big time. Although Don's mom wouldn't let him see the Ottawa show, she saw the passion that her son held for both Elvis and this new rock and roll music. She bought Don his first guitar at Ormes Furniture on Sparks Street shortly after the Sullivan show. "I haven't put it down since," Don told me. His persistence paid off, as Don Norman became one of Ottawa's top stars in the '60s with The Esquires and Don Norman and the Other Four.

Butch Pro was lucky enough to see Elvis in Ottawa. The young drummer for a new band called The Talkabouts forked out his $2.00 for a ticket. "That show put rock and roll out front," he says. "The city kind of came to life and everybody was talking about it. We were able to get in the cheap seats. It was just unreal, the electricity in the air. Everybody was so wound up. It was loud. When you are in a fever pitch, you just go with the flow, you don't listen to the words. It was just to see the appearance and people just going wild."

The audience that night was a mix of hysterical young girls, their dates (who wanted to see what the Presley kid had) and pretty well every musician in town, all curious to sample this new style of music that was grabbing all the headlines. The scene backstage was in stark contrast to the fever pitch building out front while the warmup acts tried desperately to attract some interest.

Elvis on stage in Ottawa (Courtesy City of Ottawa Archives)

CFRA disc jockey Gord Atkinson was the master of ceremonies that night and found Elvis didn't quite live up to his billing as the delinquent corrupter of young souls. Atkinson described Elvis as "the nicest kid, a real country boy. I think he was totally overwhelmed by everything that had happened. I was lucky enough to get an interview with him, and I walked into this hockey dressing room and he's sitting on a folding chair. It's the most unglamorous setting that you could possibly think of, and he has a glass of milk in one hand and a ham sandwich in the other. It didn't even have lettuce! And he couldn't get out, because if he'd walked out the door, the kids would have absolutely been all over him. He called me 'sir' all through the interview. He was a very nice young man, totally in contrast to what the parents thought."

After the second show, Elvis and his entourage retired to the "luxury" of the downtown Beacon Arms Hotel, where his famous pink Cadillac was parked out of sight in the underground lot. The next morning it was off to Philadelphia to prepare for a two-day stand. The third and final Canadian show would have to wait till late August, when he played for more than 26,000 fans—the largest crowd for an entertainment event in the history of Canada!

Ottawa got "The King" at the peak of his power. 1956 had been an historic year for Elvis Presley and North American society as a whole. He had just signed an incredible deal with RCA Records, received good reviews for his first starring role in the movie *Love Me Tender*, and just before he headed north, Elvis had purchased a new property in Memphis that he called Graceland. There was no question he was rivalling Frank Sinatra as the #1 entertainer in the world.

What started as a local phenomenon in Memphis in July 1954 had turned into a nationwide "mania" by 1956. His first tour of the southwestern states had made converts of young musicians like Buddy Holly, Dewey Cox and Roy Orbison, and his appearances on the Dorsey Brothers' *Stage Show*, *The Milton Berle Show*, *The Steve Allen Show*, and then, most famously, *The Ed Sullivan Show* in September 1956, brought Elvis to the world via the relatively new medium of television. A generation of young kids watched in awe as the girls screamed and wept at the feet of this handsome, slightly dangerous-looking former truck driver.

Elvis fans line up to see The King on the silver screen, 1956
(Courtesy City of Ottawa Archives)

And the fact that parents and other authority figures described it as "the Devil's music" didn't hurt either. It's no secret that pressure from the Roman Catholic Church was instrumental in banning Elvis Presley from playing in Montreal in 1957. That didn't stop more than five hundred Montreal fans from jumping aboard a train dubbed "The Presley Express."

Students in Roman Catholic schools in Ottawa were threatened with suspension if they dared go to the show. Indeed, eight girls from Notre Dame Convent School who attended the Ottawa show were expelled.

These poor souls had broken their written promise not to attend, which had been written on classroom blackboards in the days before the concert. It read: "I promise that I shall not take part in the reception accorded Elvis Presley, and I shall not be present at the program presented by him at the Auditorium on Wednesday, April 3, 1957." The girls had to copy this down, sign on the bottom, and hand in the notes to their teachers. There are also apocryphal tales of young girls slipping out the upstairs window to see Elvis against the explicit orders of their parents.

John Lennon once said, "Before Elvis, there was nothing." That may have been true in Liverpool and other British outposts, but here in North America, the music scene of the early '50s was anything but barren. There wouldn't have been an Elvis without Hank Williams, Big Joe Turner and even the under-appreciated Bill Haley. And while it can be argued whether Elvis was a true "rock and roller," his incredible success set the table for Jerry Lee Lewis, Little Richard, Chuck Berry and the first wave of rockers.

The fire had been lit, and Ottawa musicians were ready to get their share of the heat!

BITS & PIECES

THAT SUIT

The official title of the 1959 album is *50,000,000 Elvis Fans Can't Be Wrong: Elvis' Gold Records, Volume 2*. The number was an estimate by his producer of how many records Elvis had sold between 1954 and 1959.

Surprisingly, the material on the record pales in comparison to the timeless tracks on Volume 1, but the material on the cover was iconic. It was all about…THE SUIT!

Elvis' gold lamé outfit represented all that was gawdy and fabulous about Elvis. It was how a "King" should dress among the common rabble.

It was actually an old picture, from early 1957. The suit had been handmade for Elvis in late 1956 at the suggestion of, who else, Colonel Tom Parker. He wanted his client to look like a megastar, and he was impressed by the incredible stage gear that country star Hank Snow wore. So, the good Colonel commissioned tailor-to-the-stars Nudie Cohen to pull out all the stops for his boy.

While it looks expensive, the process of creating a lamé suit wasn't that difficult. They took a regular suit and added strips of a gold or silver ribbon around it. The suit cost about $500 to make, although the Colonel claimed it was worth about $10,000.

Elvis probably hated it, but went along with the stunt. He wore it a couple of times on stage in 1957 but found it to be hot and not at all suited to his gyrations. He also didn't think it was flattering for his figure.

Nevertheless, "The Suit" was in the luggage when Elvis took off for Canadian concerts in April. He wore the whole outfit for his first show in Toronto, with the jacket, the tie, the belt and the shoes, along with black pants. He dropped the gold tie for the second Toronto show and the Ottawa concerts. By the time he reached Philadelphia later in the tour, "The Suit" was in storage, and Elvis looked a lot more comfortable.

In 1968, producers of the legendary Elvis comeback TV show wanted Elvis to break out the gold outfit for old times' sake. Today you can see the original gold lamé outfit behind glass at Graceland. It's estimated to worth over two million dollars. And it still looks damned uncomfortable!

BEFORE ELVIS

The Parkways. L-R: Wayne Tender, Carol Corbeau, Bob Hanni, Lennie Leitch

In the mid- to late '50s, Ottawa was like any other North American mid-size city when it came to nightlife. There were dance clubs where kids could "jive" the night away to the sounds of travelling big bands or local orchestras that would play the hits of the day from the hot vocal groups or "girl" singers. On any given Friday or Saturday, spots like the Centertown Ballroom at Bank and Somerset, Lakeside Gardens at Britannia Beach, Standish Hall in Gatineau, The Rideau Ferry Inn between Smiths Falls and Perth, The Glenlea Golf Club, the legendary Chaudière just over the bridge and other Quebec clubs in Quyon, Thurso, Shawville and Buckingham, would be hopping to the strains of local acts like Berkley Kidd and his Orchestra, The Parkways, The Playdates, The Imperials, The Hi-Tones, Wayne (Latendresse) Tender, The Showmen and The Starlighters, or travelling artists like Tommy Dorsey, Woody Herman, Louis Armstrong, Stan Kenton, Buddy Rich, Tony Bennett and Frankie Avalon. Avalon was so impressed with The Talkabouts that he arranged a recording session for them in New York City.

Wayne (Latendresse) Tender

Smaller combos specializing in playing the hits by The Four Aces, The Fours Lads, etc. also had their spaces to entertain the younger crowd.

Out in the Valley, it was a different world. When DJ Dean Hagopian arrived here from London, Ontario, in 1960, he stepped into a music scene that was totally unique. "The Ottawa Valley was more country on both sides of the border, the Quebec side and the Ontario side. Even on CFRA, Mac Beattie and the Happy Wanderers were huge, absolutely huge. There weren't that many groups around and those that were, were heavily themed towards country. A lot of rock influence was with these country bands, like Hugh Scott. There's a guy who should have gone places, and another guy named Maury Logan," says Dean.

Valley legends The Happy Wanderers

Butch Pro played drums for The Talkabouts. As a drummer he was drawn to the driving beat of rock and roll the first time he heard "Rock Around the Clock" by Bill Haley and the Comets.

Before Elvis, The Talkabouts had played pop hits from The Four Aces, The Four Lads and other lightweight combos. After seeing Elvis, they became more of a rock and roll band, and a few months later became the first "rock" band to play at the prestigious Chaudière Club in Hull in the legendary "Green Door" room.

The Talkabouts

ROCKIN' ON THE RIDEAU

Butch Pro sees April 3, 1957 as a turning point for the Ottawa music scene: "The next year all the local dance clubs were really coming into play. Out at Lakeside Garden in Britannia, the big bands started playing some upbeat stuff too."

Rock and roll bands also found gigs in unlikely venues, like bowling alleys, restaurants and movie theatres. The Talkabouts had a regular two-night-a-week gig at the Francais Theatre on Dalhousie. Maury Logan did his "Elvis" routine at the Standish Hall in Hull, between movies at the Rideau Theatre and even at drive-ins, where he would perform on top of the snack shack between flicks.

To be fair, it wasn't only Elvis who brought this new energy and life to the Ottawa music scene. Dave Britten, another member of The Talkabouts from Lisgar High, says, "I saw Buddy Holly when he came to town. I saw all those 'big shows' of '57, '58 and '59 at the Auditorium. The Crickets, Eddie Cochrane, The Everly Brothers, Paul Anka and Jerry Lee Lewis. It was just ongoing rock and roll."

Jerry Lee Lewis at the Auditorium, 1958

THE BEAT GOES ON: 1957 – 1963

Guitar-rock with The Strangers.
Future Esquire Gary Comeau far right.

Although rock and roll made newspaper headlines in the late '50s, it wasn't always for the best of reasons. Elvis was drafted, Buddy Holly died in a plane crash a few weeks after a concert in Ottawa, Chuck Berry went to jail and Little Richard quit music and entered the Christian ministry. And then there was the scandal involving Jerry Lee Lewis marrying his thirteen-year-old cousin.

By 1960, as many critics had predicted, rock and roll was essentially dead and buried. But dig down a bit deeper and there were some real nuggets in the mud, and it was the music that kids were listening to.

Between 1958 and 1963, The Kingston Trio had five #1 albums in North America and nine more in the Top 10. They led the so-called "folk revival," along with the Rooftop Singers; The Serendipity Singers; Trini Lopez; The

Brothers Four, who leaned more towards songs of the Old West; Peter, Paul and Mary; and the New Christy Minstrels, whose roots went back to the post-Civil War days.

While the general public ate up the folk revival sound, purists like Ottawa's Sandy Crawley turned up their noses at this "commercial folk" and opted for true folk singers like Woody Guthrie, Phil Ochs, and this new kid from Minnesota who changed his name from Robert Zimmerman to Bob Dylan. It's safe to say that before The Beatles came over, the most popular music form in Ottawa, next to country, was folk music, and the place to hang out was Le Hibou Coffee House.

In 1959, a young singer/songwriter from Detroit named Barry Gordy borrowed $800 and started up a record company he wanted to call Tammy Records after a big hit song of the day. That name was taken, so he settled Tamla Records. Later that year, he spun off another label called Motown. It became one of the few American musical projects to thrive during the British Invasion, thanks to huge cross-over hits from the Supremes, The Temptations, Stevie Wonder, Marvin Gaye and others.

The sound of '50s rock was kept alive by The Beach Boys, who tapped into the surf fad on the West Coast by mixing the basic rock and roll of Chuck Berry with the guitar-based, driving sound of guitar legends Dick Dale and Link Wray.

Their amazing string of hits began with "Surfin'" in 1961 and didn't let up till 1967, weathering the British Invasion and the Summer of Love.

The Beach Boys play a high school dance in 1962

And then there were the boys and their guitars!

Duane Eddy started playing guitar when he was five. By the time he was twenty, Duane was one of the most popular recording artists in America, thanks to his producer/co-writer Lee Hazlewood and a "twangy" guitar sound accentuated by studio echo effects. Featuring a screaming sax solo, "Rebel Rouser" was Eddy's first smash in 1958, followed by "Ramrod," "Peter Gunn," "Because They're Young" and many others. His albums were the perfect fodder for young kids who were trying to figure out their first chords.

Duane Eddy: The King of Twang

Must-haves for guitar-rock fans were the works of The Ventures and The Shadows, who competed for the instrumental crown on different sides of the Atlantic. The Shadows were also singer Cliff Richard's backing band, but attained such respect that they reached the same sales level with their own records in the U.K. The band was a classic four-piece with two guitars, bass and drums. Lead player Hank Marvin belongs near the top of any guitar-player poll. His nerdish looks belied his abilities as a consummate musician, and like Eddy, he inspired a generation of kids to pick up and, more importantly, practise on those six string devils.

Cliff Richard and The Shadows

The Shadows, sadly, didn't get much radio play on this side of Atlantic. That role was snatched by The Ventures from Tacoma, Washington. Along with Buddy Holly, Chuck Berry, Duane Eddy, Link Wray and others, The Ventures made the guitar the coolest thing about rock and roll. If you're a guitar player and you don't know how to play "Walk Don't Run," I suggest you get on YouTube right now start working on it. At one point in 1963, just before you-know-who arrived, The Ventures had five albums in the Billboard Top 100 and guitar sales hit a record high.

Famed British producer Joe Meek wrote and produced the instrumental "Telstar" in 1962, which reached #1 in both Britain and North America. Named for the recently launched telecommunications satellite, "Telstar" is considered to be the first "sci-fi" rock song, and featured Joe's studio house band The Tornados. Like most other British and American instrumental bands, the wind went out of The Tornados' sails the next year when The Beatles buried instrumental rock as a major commercial force.

Less guitar-driven was Johnny and the Hurricanes from Toledo, Ohio. Their specialty was taking old standard tunes and setting them to a rock and roll beat. They turned the cowboy song "Red River Valley" into "Red River Rock," for example, and had a huge hit with the update in 1959. Instead of relying on just the twangy guitars, Johnny and the Hurricanes shone the spotlight on their organ and sax players, creating a different flavour for the genre.

And there were many other instrumental bands who topped the charts without the aid of lyrics. The Champs had "Tequila." My favourite was "Wild Weekend" by the Rockin' Rebels from Buffalo, New York. That song cracked the Top 10 in 1961.

The reign of instrumental rock was a golden era not only for the guitar, but for the saxophone as well. Hits like "Wild Weekend," "Rebel Rouser" and "Tequila" all featured sax solos, and players like King Curtis and Boots Randolph became stars. The Dave Clark Five was the only British Invasion band to have a sax player, as most bands relied more on the two guitars, bass and drums format. Still, in the late '50s, mainly instrumental bands with sax and organ were common, even here in Ottawa.

THE HI-TONES

Judging by the packed houses, the most popular rock and roll band in Ottawa in late '50s was The Hi-Tones. Bob St. George was their guitar player. "It was the time of Duane Eddy with sax and guitar, and we started out playing instrumentals by him and Johnny and the Hurricanes and other instrumental groups. The vocal pieces we'd do were "hit parade" songs from Dion, Buddy Holly and other stars of the day. So live we'd play maybe two instrumentals and then I'd sing a song or two and then back to more instrumentals."

When Elvis came to town in 1957, Bob was one of many young musicians who snatched up tickets. Elvis was the focal point of course, but for Bob, "The King" was the secondary attraction. He says, "The first reason I got into playing guitar was Scotty Moore, who played guitar for Elvis. It wasn't Elvis that inspired me to play, it was Scotty."

Bob was introduced to brothers Don and Bill Billows by a friend who also played guitar. They invited him to play guitar with their band The Hi-Tones, but only if he learned to sing. The band was mainly instrumental, but the Billows boys knew they had to throw in some vocal ballads to keep the girls happy.

Being too young to play in the clubs, when the band was ready to play in front of people they took a DIY approach, according to Bob. "We would just drop by community centre dances on Saturday night and ask if we could play a few songs. If they said yes, we'd play the three songs we knew and then head out to another community centre and do the same thing. That's how we got started as a live band. Then we started going to talent competitions on the Hull side. That was tough, 'cause you could never beat the little kids. Next, we started doing some high school dances and actually got paid. Then we started making our own dances at the Midtown Ballroom, which was above the Beamish store at Bank and Somerset. I think it was Big Bud's after that. It had bingo some nights and the guy would have bands on other nights. So, we auditioned, and we got a gig on a Friday night. It went so well that we did that on a regular basis. We played there Tuesday-Saturday. The cover charge was $1. When we played the Midtown, it was always packed. They were lined up down the stairs."

The Hi-Tones had become Ottawa's top rock and roll band. With an organ and sax, they had the sound that was popular on the radio, and a look that was both hip and professional. "When we first started, we wore black pants with tiger-striped sweaters," says Bob. "Then we bought suits with black pants, and a blue jacket with a tie and a red jacket with a matching tie. We'd play a set in the blue jacket and one with the red."

The suits were needed for the supper and dance clubs that were mostly on the Quebec side. At the time, several swanky golf courses doubled as dance halls on the weekends, and bands like The Hi-Tones, The Talkabouts, The Playdates, The Starlighters, the Regals, Morgan McReynolds and The Barons made great money hitting the clubs from Aylmer to Thurso and far beyond, including a club in Angers called the Hotel Royal owned by Nick Anka, Paul's cousin. Musicians called the joint "Chez Nick," and it was a regular stop for The Hi-Tones.

The Morgan McReynolds Trio

One gig Bob remembers well was at the Hull Arena where The Hi-Tones pulled double duty. "We did our own show, and then we backed up a young singer named Gordie Lightfoot. He was a folk singer and it wasn't going too well for him, so he put out a pop ballad called 'Remember Me'. It was his way of trying to get popular. We practised the song with him in the dressing room and went out and played it. He only sang two songs. Then he became a big star with his folk music."

There was also the night they opened a show at Lansdowne Park for an up-and-coming young American singer named Chubby Checker, who was just climbing the charts with his first single "The Twist." Backstage after the show, Chubby showed Hi-Tones drummer Lennie Leitch how to do the dance.

But for Hi-Tones fans, the band is best remembered for their lengthy stint at their "home club," the Oak Door on Band near Argyle. The owner of the building was having trouble finding a new tenant, so the Billow brothers offered to rent out the spot for weekend dances. They were an instant success, and it wasn't long before fans were lined up the stairs to get in, just like at the Midtown Ballroom. And with the notorious Post brothers handling the security, the Oak Door rivalled Pineland as the place to be for rock and roll.

The Oak Door, 1963

Don Billows took over as manager of the Oak Door and started booking bands all over town through his own agency, Don Billows Progressive Group Management. Two of his hottest acts were Eastern Passage and The Heart. He said he had a hard time finding enough bands to fill all the venues.

But it wasn't only The Hi-Tones at the Oak Door. With a capacity of 1,200, soon they could afford to bring in other acts. The most popular was, hands down, Ronnie Hawkins and the Hawks from Toronto.

"Rompin' Ronnie" was born in Arkansas but fell in love with Canada during his early trips up here at a singer. He relocated to Toronto, where he quickly became a staple on the entertainment strip. The only member of his original Hawks to stay in Toronto with him was drummer Levon Helm. The other spots in the group were filled by Canadians Robbie Robertson, Garth Hudson, Richard Manuel and Rick Danko, later know as simply "The Band."

Most performers who saw Ronnie and the Hawks play live could pick up a million pointers about being a performer and a professional musician. Bob St. George certainly did. "When Ronnie Hawkins and the Hawks came to town, every guitarist and every band was there. They were so far ahead of every band out there. Everybody was taken aback by the sound

Robbie Robertson used to get on his guitar. And Garth Hudson is probably the best organ player I ever heard in my life."

Another huge attraction at the Oak Door was a band from Montreal called The Sceptres, leaders of the red hot "yé-yé" sound in Quebec. Yé-yé bands made their mark by taking American hits and recording them in French. For example, one of The Sceptres' biggest tunes was "Enfin Seul Ensemble," a French take on "I Think We're Alone Now" by Tommy James and the Shondells. Promoted as Quebec's first bilingual band, The Sceptres found huge audiences on both sides of the Ottawa River.

The Sceptres

The Beau-Marks from Montreal were also regulars at the Oak Door. Their mega-hit "Clap Your Hands" topped charts around the world in 1960, and that year they became the second Canadian rock and roll act to appear on *The Ed Sullivan Show*. The first were The Crew Cuts from Toronto of "Sh-Boom, Sh-Boom" fame in 1957.

Taking into account the Ballroom shows, two nights at week at the Aylmer Bowling Lanes and the Oak Door residency, at their peak The Hi-Tones were working six nights a week. But the times were about to change, big time. New groups like The Esquires and The Barons were starting at attract bigger crowds with their fresh sounds and looks. But the big reckoning came one day when Bob recalls their manager walking into the room with a new record tucked under his arm. "It was *Beatlemania*. He said we should listen to it because they were going to be popular. The problem was we only had one singer in the band and their songs had lots of harmonies. That's why a band like The Hi-Tones struggled around then, because we couldn't do Beatles songs. People didn't want to hear Buddy Holly and Duane Eddy anymore. Brian Lewicki and The Barons were different. When Brian sang a Rolling Stones song you would swear it was the Stones. Or if he sang a Beatles song he sounded like The Beatles. We couldn't do that."

It was in with the new and out with the old. The Hi-Tones members drifted off to other projects. Drummer Lennie Leitch started booking the new breed of Ottawa bands using the name Lennie Alexander.

Although they didn't leave an Elvis-style legacy in Ottawa, The Hi-Tones did make their mark on the Ottawa rock and roll scene, which was in its infancy. Brian Lewicki of the Barons, Esquires and MRQ says seeing The Hi-Tones at a dance at Commerce High in 1958 or 1959 made him want to "do that." In a fuzzy black-and-white photo of an early Hi-Tones gig, you can spot a young man in a suit standing beside the stage, checking out the band. It was Richard Patterson of The Electrons and later of The Esquires, Three's a Crowd and Canada Goose. And The Hi-Tones were the first Ottawa rock band to record an album, 1961's "Hi Jump" on the Montaigne label.

Bob St. George summed it up nicely with this story: "I put some pictures of the Oak Door on Facebook recently and this girl wrote back and said, 'my mother and father first met at the Oak Door.' I told her chances were I talked to them there. Those were such good times."

THE JIVE ROCKETS

The Jive Rockets: George, Dewey, Ralph and Vern

If anyone can rightfully lay claim to the title "Ottawa's First Rock and Roll Band," it would be the Jive Rockets.

The Jive Rockets were formed by a young country music fan named Ralph Carlson in 1955. The first lineup was Carlson on guitar, Paul Anka's cousin Bob Anka on Bass, and drummer Dewey Midkiff.

The material the band played was that hybrid of country and jump blues that would be tagged "rockabilly," along with the hits of the day and some straight country, which was *the* sound of the Ottawa Valley.

A slightly later lineup featured Ralph and some friends from Commerce High School, guitarist Vern Craig, and a bit later, drummer Jack MacDonald. Jack took over the drumming chores from Midkiff, who had decided to try his luck in Nashville as a sideman and studio musician. He changed his name to Dewey Martin, toured with Patsy Cline, The Everly Brothers and other country stars and then went west and hooked up with a band called Buffalo Springfield, named for a company that made steamrollers.

The Jive Rockets were already gigging frequently when they graduated from high school. They moved from school dances to club gigs before landing a plum residency on the Quebec side.

In the late '50s, Hugh Scott just about owned the Chamberland Hotel stage. He and his band the Meteors were the house band there from Wednesday to Saturday for an amazing thirteen years. The other two nights were filled by other bands, including the Jive Rockets, who made such an impression they did that slot for six months.

The Jive Rockets on stage at the Chamberland Hotel, 1961

The Jive Rockets always drew a crowd, and Jack MacDonald says that included a lot of area musicians: "We were the first rock and roll band in Ottawa. There aren't many people who recognize that fact. I know for a fact I was the first young drummer playing around town. Then came Ricky Patterson. He would come around to our shows and watch the band. Don Norman from The Esquires would come by and watch us play all the time, and he told me that's what helped him decide to get into a band."

The band also took a DIY approach to gigs, as had The Hi-Tones with their stint at the Oak Door. "At one point we rented the hall up in Chesterville on Saturday nights," Jack told me. We'd drive out there, hire a security guard and someone to sell tickets and we just had dances. It was a steady Saturday night gig for us, and we make lots of money. We should have moved into the club scene more quickly than we did. Perhaps if we had hooked up with someone who had known the ins and outs of the business, it might have been different."

When Vern and Jack MacDonald jumped to another band, the Jive Rockets were done. "Vern and I met Dean Hagopian, the DJ from CKOY," says Jack. "That was how The Staccatos were born. Vern and I thought it would be great with Dean because of all his connections. We got a lot of exposure because of that. I left the band in the early '60s, just before they started to get well known. I had just gotten a government job in Ottawa, and on my father's advice I quit music and stayed with that job. I loved those days and playing with those bands, but I never regretted that decision."

Perhaps it was a lack of that guiding promotional touch that hurt the legacy of the Jive Rockets, but there is no doubting their place in our story. They are the band that bridged that transition period in popular music from the male singing groups to the hip-shaking rock and rollers.

The Jive Rockets were regulars on Gord Atkinson's *Campus Hop*, as were The Hi-Tones. The Rockets placed first in the third CFRA Campus Hop at the Coliseum in November 1958, playing material by Jerry Lee Lewis and Elvis. If you're keeping score at home, in second spot were the Rhythm Rockers from Hull with Jerry and the Rhythm Boys third.

At the first Campus Hop, the Jive Rockets placed second, beaten out by a kid from Fisher Park High School who did a mean Elvis Presley impression. His name was Hughie Scott.

HUGHIE SCOTT

"I started the whole shebang."

Blink and you might miss Riceville, Ontario. It's one of many small towns scattered along the back roads of the Ottawa Valley. Towns like Riceville are a source of intense pride for Ottawans, who embrace the rural heritage of the nation's capital city. The Valley has always had its own language, a strong sense of community, and its own musical heritage.

Populated mainly by Scottish, Irish, English, and French settlers, Valley music traditionally mixed Celtic, folk and Gaelic music driven by fiddles, guitars, step-dancing and big smiles. In the '50s, regional stars like Mac Beattie and The Melodiers, Valley DJ Ted Daigle and The Happy Wanderers, fronted by "Papa" Joe Brown, packed dance halls and taverns up and down the Valley. This was the music that Hugh Scott grew up with.

Before starting up CKBY-FM, Ted Daigle was a rockabilly star in the Valley

Hugh and his family moved to Ottawa in 1953. He was thirteen years old and already well known in the Valley because of his skills as a fiddle player. He calls it "a gift from God," but it took a lot of plain, hard work and blisters to learn to play guitar. Like many young kids before and after him, Hughie Scott spent countless hours in front of the mirror, lip-syncing to Elvis Presley's "Mystery Train," and the songs of Hank Williams, Hank Snow, and his idol, Jerry Lee Lewis.

At fifteen, he and his buddies would sneak into the Chamberland Hotel in Aylmer to see Smokey Rand and the Drifters. His persistence paid off when Smokey allowed him on stage to do his take on Jerry Lee Lewis and Bill Haley. And when Bill Haley and the Comets came to town to play the Rose Room at the Chaudière, you can guess who was right up in front of the stage. Hughie Scott was learning from the masters.

Hughie went to Fisher Park High School, which was no different than any other school of the time in North America. The girls had Elvis pin-ups in their lockers, and the boys all combed their hair like Elvis and copped "rebel" attitudes in the hallways. But Hugh Scott went one better: he could *be* Elvis. Those hours of practising in front of the mirror had paid off, and by his second year, he was well known for his Elvis impersonations, almost as well known as another boy singer at Fisher Park named Paul Anka, who was also a member of the singing trio The Bobby Soxers. "Every Friday afternoon there would be an assembly," remembers Hugh. "We'd all get up there, and nobody could stand Paul. Paul asked me to come up and play guitar with him, but my friends said they never talk to me again if I did it."

Talent night at the Fairmont Hotel in Hull, 1956. Pierette Dupont (left) channels Elvis, but is no match for your winner, Ottawa's own singing sensation, fifteen-year-old Paul Anka (right). Less than a year later, Anka would be the hottest singer in North America on the release of "Diana." (Courtesy The Jean-Marc Carisse collection)

Anka would go south and become a superstar, but back home there were no gold records for Hughie Scott. But he was knocking audiences dead with his Elvis routine and rockabilly songs with Smokey and the Drifters at the Chamberland, the British Hotel and the Aylmer Hotel. He had become a big deal, and that's the way the Valley boy liked it.

His ability to channel Elvis won him a spot on Gord Atkinson's *Campus Hop*, and as he remembers it, the reaction was pretty similar too. "The girls chased me into the bathroom. They had to call in extra security. They all had their hands out trying to grab me."

By the time he was seventeen, Hughie had two bands on the go, playing on the Quebec side from the Chaud and Glenlea Golf Club down to the

Aylmer strip. For thirteen years, Hughie Scott and the Meteors played seven nights a week at the Chamberland Hotel in Aylmer. Every night was packed. When he moved down the road for a residency at the Chaudière, Hughie Scott became the second top money-making performer in the country! He also enjoyed a guest stint in Vern Craig's rockabilly band the Jive Rockets. When it came to rock and roll in this area, Hughie Scott was The Man.

He had four albums and thirteen singles make the local and national charts, played on the *Tommy Hunter Show* on CBC and hobnobbed with Ronnie Hawkins and country superstar Waylon Jennings, who offered to bring Hughie down to Vegas to open for him. Hughie turned him down, although Jennings told him he "could be the next Willie Nelson." Better to be a star back home than just another face on the buses along the backroads of America.

Hughie's band offered a staging ground for many great local players. Les Emmerson and Vern Craig both played guitar for *The Hughie Scott Show* prior to The Staccatos. Before he headed south to join fellow Canadians Bruce Palmer and Neil Young in Buffalo Springfield, Dewey Martin from Chesterville was his drummer.

Rather than ignore the changing times, Hughie added a few Beatles songs to his repertoire when the British Invasion hit in '64, although he faithfully relied on his bread and butter…'50s rockabilly and rock and roll.

I only saw Hughie perform once, and that was at a rock and roll reunion show at the Chaud. He was seventy-two years old, but still put on as energetic a show as he must have in the late 1950s at the Chamberland Hotel. He is a flat-out rock and roll legend because, as he says himself, "I was the one who started the whole shebang."

And so we entered a new decade. In most ways, the early 1960s were just an extension of the '50s. Radio played a bland mix of romantic pop, novelty songs and fresh-faced young stars who were as wholesome as apple pie. The first wave of Baby Boomers were now teenagers, and they were getting bored, just as their older brothers and sisters had been when Elvis smashed through in 1956.

In 1964, it happened again, and this time, on an even bigger scale.

SANDY GARDINER AND BEATLEMANIA

In September 1963, about five months before the *Ed Sullivan Show* appearance, Sandy Gardiner wrote his famous "Beatlemania" article, the first time that term would be used in North America.

It's ironic that two years before the British Invasion swamped North America and changed the look and sound of popular music, a recently arrived Scotsman had pretty well the same effect on Ottawa.

Sandy Gardiner was a Scottish journalist who also wrote for the prestigious British music magazine the *New Music Express*. His job mostly entailed interviewing touring American musicians and keeping an ear to the ground for new homegrown talent.

When he emigrated to Canada in 1962, the whispers about this tight little band from Liverpool called The Beatles were just starting to be heard throughout the U.K. "Beatlemania" proper was still about a year away, but whenever he went home to visit, Sandy would deliver updates for his Ottawa audience.

When he arrived here, Sandy recalls the music scene was "low key." The tide of youthful exuberance over rock bands like The Beatles hadn't reached this side of the Atlantic yet, but Sandy knew it wouldn't be long. In fact, newspapers like the *Ottawa Journal* didn't really care much about the youth culture, because kids don't buy newspapers. But with some good salesmanship, he persuaded the *Journal* editor to give him a full page on Saturdays just for the kids.

"Platter Patter and Idol Chatter" covered the youth scene, from the hottest fashions to what was happening on the local and international music scenes. Gradually the music took over, and every Saturday we would read that page to find out what was happening in Ottawa and, more interestingly, England.

While The Beatles and the Stones were on the stage getting the accolades, there were others standing in the wings analyzing their every move and planning the next step.

These Svengalis were the managers, exclusively men back then, who handled the business end of a tough and still new form of entertainment. There were no set rules, but legends like "Colonel" Tom Parker, Brian Epstein and Andrew Loog-Oldham were great role models for those to come.

"Colonel" Tom had taken Elvis Presley to the tippy-top of the highest peaks in showbiz, first with music, then movies and then his final role as "The King." Brian Epstein had ventured down to the clammy basement of The Cavern Club in Liverpool to catch a young band called The Silver Beatles. He put the leather-clad kids into suits and ties and made them a fortune. Loog-Oldham did the reverse. He encouraged his charges The Rolling Stones to be anything but nice and clean. That worked pretty well too.

Sandy Gardiner was quite familiar with Brian and Andrew. He was there while the Stones and Beatles were making their climb. He brought that knowledge to Ottawa, and, as a manager to Ottawa's biggest bands, he made it work more than once.

SOME "IDOL CHATTER" WITH SANDY GARDINER

Platter Patter
... And Idol Chatter
By Sandy Gardiner

JH: How did a Scottish music writer end up in Ottawa?

SG: Originally, I was a rock journalist working for newspapers in Scotland. I also wrote for the *New Musical*

Express in the U.K., which, at that time, was the British equivalent of *Billboard Magazine*. When the top artists from the States came through the U.K., I would interview them for the magazine. I came to Ottawa in 1962. When I came to the *Journal* they had no youth coverage at all. The music scene to them was totally foreign. So, I suggested to the managing editor that at least once a week, on a Saturday, we should dedicate a full page of features that would be interesting to youth, but also hung around the music scene. And I started doing a column for them and interviews for them, many of which had appeared in the *New Music Express* in England. It was called "Platter Patter and Idol Chatter."

JH: Now you were managing local bands at the time. Was there a little conflict of interest going on there?

SG: Maybe, but I did my best to support all the bands. After a while, other groups came looking for me to help them with advice or direction, and I did work with The Townsmen, The Scoundrelz and The Characters along with The Esquires and Staccatos. This was all in my spare time. I was a busy guy. I worked from six in the morning till two in the afternoon and then moved into the music role in the afternoon.

JH: Legend has it you are the guy who coined the tag "Beatlemania" in North America. How did that come about?

SG: I would continue to go back and forth from Canada to the U.K., and on one particular trip when I was there, it was pretty obvious that there was a new band on the British scene who was beginning to emerge as the first real serious challenger to the American domination of the U.K. charts. Having seen them perform there, I wrote the article titled "Beatlemania" for the *Ottawa Journal* in September 1963. And as a result of that title, it also became the title of their Canadian album, which in the U.K. was called *With the Beatles*.

JH: You obviously saw a growing movement in rock and roll in England. Is that why you decided to get into the scene over here?

SG: The music scene when I arrived in Ottawa was pretty much low key. It was in its infancy. I could see that there was a real void there. There weren't really any Canadian bands breaking through the clutter, it was all U.S. dominated. So I thought to myself, wouldn't it be an interesting challenge to see if I could start with a Canadian band and get them to have a hit first of all in Canada. And the first group I worked with was The Esquires. Of course, they were heavily influenced by Cliff Richard and The Shadows. The other bands in Ottawa at the time all sounded like the top American acts. And with The Esquires we did succeed in having a couple of hits while I was involved with them. And then I was approached by a member of The Staccatos about possibly managing them and looking after their recording career. I knew there was a lot of work to be done, but the band had a lot of potential, and the rest is pretty much history. It took about four years to break out for them. Each record sold more and more until finally it got to the ultimate record, which was "Signs."

JH: What do you remember about the area clubs at the time?

SG: Ronnie Hawkins was a very popular performer at the time. His backup band the Hawks would turn into "The Band" in a few years and back up Dylan. There were a bunch of clubs that had the Yanks coming through. The Ottawa House was one. They seemed to have a lot of travelling bands come through. The Townsmen played there as well, and a number of other bands. But the main club was the Chaudière in Hull. Of course, over there you could buy drinks because the drinking age was lower. And you were allowed to smoke, so there was always a pall of smoke hanging over the place. So it was a different atmosphere to begin with. The Staccatos were the house band for a while. Pineland was one of the few places in Ottawa where you could really showcase a band. That's where The Esquires started.

THE ESQUIRES

Still photo from The Esquires'
"Man From Adano" video.

Richard Patterson had a rule of thumb when The Esquires played Pineland. If the cars were lined up illegally down Riverside Drive, it was going to be a good night. Most nights, the tail-lights went on for miles.

The Esquires were the first band to make a major impact on the Ottawa rock and roll scene of the 1960s.

Most bands of the time patterned their sound after the big American artists of rock and roll and doo-wop, but The Esquires were influenced heavily by British pop star Cliff Richard, and even more so by his cracking backup band, The Shadows.

The Shadows are remembered by most North American music fans as the band that backed up Britain's answer to Elvis, pretty-boy Harry Webb, better known by his stage name, Cliff Richard. But calling them just a "backup band" would be selling the band far short. The Shadows were, in fact, the first British band to dominate the British pop charts, with timeless instrumentals like "Apache," "Man of Mystery" and "F.B.I." Fuelled by guitar virtuosos Hark Marvin and Bruce Welch, the "Shads" were the top rock and roll band in pre-Beatles Britain, and rivalled America's Ventures as the top instrumental band in the world, all the time working behind Richard. They developed dance routines to make up for Richard's awkward stage presence and dressed in matching suits and ties that would set the fashion standard for The Beatles, Gerry and the Pacemakers and countless other British Invasion bands.

But while The Shadows and Cliff became huge stars in Britain, they were virtually unknown and unheard in North America. So how did a Shadows record end up on the record player in Clint Hierlihy's Ottawa bedroom in 1960? It was simply a case of vinyl immigration.

Clint's dad was in the Canadian Forces and served several stints in England. When he'd come home, he'd bring back the hottest British hits for his son, the music fan. Clint would share the exotic tunes with his buddy Gary Comeau, who lived down the street. The two kids loved the jam to the music, with Clint on bass and Gary on guitar.

Comeau, despite his youth, was already a veteran on the Ottawa band scene. "I started playing guitar in 1957 after seeing Buddy Holly at the Coliseum in 1957. I started listening to his records and buying them… The sound of the guitar was so different and so unique. So it was like, 'Oh wow, how to do you do that?'" he recalls. "Presley's stuff was all right, but I didn't find it that moving, whereas the early Buddy Holly stuff was really, really cool…The Fender guitar sound is the key motivator there. I went to see a local band called the Jive Rockets, with Vern Craig and Hughie Scott. My parents got me a guitar for Christmas from Orme's on Sparks Street, and the kid across the street started teaching me some chords. That was it!" Gary had the bug.

One day, while he was banging out some of those chords in garage, a kid walked by and asked if he wanted to be in a band. The kid's name was Clint Hierlihy. He played bass for the Fairmonts.

A name picked at random from the Ottawa phone book marked the birth of the Fairmonts in 1958. "We played almost every Friday and Saturday, and a lot of Sundays at every church hall, high school and bowling alley in Ottawa," says Gary. The Fairmonts became The Strangers in 1959, and continued to ride the local circuit before landing a dream summer-long gig in Maniwaki. There were trips to Montreal to cut some records, but gradually

The Strangers just fell apart like so many other groups. Gary passed the time jamming with Clint and waiting for the next chance to be a rock star. He got that chance with Ottawa's first great rock and roll band of the 1960s.

Inspired by the sounds of The Shadows, Gary and Clint started up a band that specialized in instrumentals with a look that mirrored their idols.

The Fairmonts with Gary Comeau (right)

The Esquires' earliest lineup featured Comeau, Hierlihy, Paul Huot on rhythm guitar, Bert Hurd on drums, and Bob Harrington, who would provide the vocals when needed. Practices were held at Gary's house.

After their first gig on the Rockcliffe airbase in 1962 came the basement shows, the all-ages clubs and community centres. The guys began to notice one particular fan showing up to gig after gig. The kid was hard not to notice. Standing about five feet tall, and just about as much around, he would stand close to the stage and absorb the sounds and stage show of The Esquires with more than a passing interest. It was like he was studying the band. The "kid" would turn out to be a drummer from another local band called The Electrons. He loved the music The Esquires were playing and was not overly subtle in his desire to join the band. It happened in March 1962, when Bert left the band and Richie Patterson took over the drum stool.

Paul Huot recalls that each member had a distinct job. "Richard was the guy who made sure the stage was okay, the lighting was okay. He was basically not only the drummer but the stage manager. Clint was in charge of the sound and Gary was the music arranger. I was a bit of a leader at the time."

It was no surprise the first single from The Esquires was an instrumental, and less of a surprise it was a cover of The Shadows' British hit, "Atlantis." The flip side was a vocal featuring Harrington, who decided to split just after the record was released.

The Esquires try to...ummm...uh...never mind.

The real game-changer was the second release. Still no vocals, but written by fellow Ottawan Dave Britten, it was called "Man from Adano." Thanks to solid radio play and the slick managerial and writing skills of Sandy Gardiner, it made #1 on the local charts and got airplay across the country, reaching the top in several cities. "So Many Other Boys" was also a sizable national hit in an era when cross-country success for a Canadian band was almost unheard of, unless you were Paul Anka or The Crew Cuts.

All-in-all, 1964 was shaping up to be a great year for the band. The Esquires were at the top of the local music food chain, although groups like the Regals, The Barons and this new group called The Staccatos were nipping at their heels. Still, The Esquires were on top and just about ready to break out across the country. And then, everything changed.

FEBRUARY 9, 1964:
LADIES AND GENTLEMEN...THE BEATLES

ED SULLIVAN (variety show host): *"Now yesterday and today our theatre's been jammed with newspapermen and hundreds of photographers from all over the nation, and these veterans agreed with me that the city never has witnessed the excitement stirred by these youngsters from Liverpool, who call themselves The Beatles. Now tonight, you're gonna twice be entertained by them. Right now, and again in the second half of our show. Ladies and gentlemen, The Beatles. Let's bring them on."*

If you take simple numbers as your determining factor, The Beatles beat Elvis!

When the Fab Four made their first appearance on *The Ed Sullivan Show* on February 9, 1964, a record 73 million Americans were tuned in. When Elvis made his 1956 debut on Sullivan, the number was around 60 million.

Taking into account the fact that fewer people owned TVs back in '56, and everybody knew who Elvis was and had already seen him on TV, let's call it a draw.

Outside of New York City, few Americans knew anything about The Beatles. Disc jockey "Murray the K" was driving the bandwagon the second the band touched down at then newly named JFK airport. Scenes from the New York arrival and hotel stay, courtesy of CBS and ABC News, beamed across the country, but still, few Americans knew what they looked or sounded like on stage. On the morning of February 10, there was little else being talked about on the streets of America, and Ottawa for that matter.

LES EMMERSON (The Staccatos): *"It was an earth-shattering moment for me, like when I first saw Elvis on TV. I knew at that moment I had to get into a band that was playing that stuff."*

GARY COMEAU (The Esquires): *"We were among the first people to hear The Beatles because our manager Sandy Gardiner brought over their records from England. We liked it because the music really different. When it hit, you could really see the bands around town, and there weren't that many, going, 'What do we do now?' The Esquires began playing Beatles music probably six months before anyone else was. We started writing stuff that was very British-sounding as well."*

BRAD CAMPBELL (The 5D): *"The catalyst for starting a band was The Beatles. Once The Beatles arrived, Dave Poulin and I had to do this for real. We were on the phone between their songs on the Sullivan show. We couldn't believe what was going on. He went out and bought a guitar. I went out and bought a guitar about two weeks later. The whole thing was just such a change from what we were used to."*

BUDDY STANTON (The Scoundrelz): *"Like most kids in Ottawa, I got into rock and roll when The Beatles arrived on the scene. I remember getting that first album and I couldn't believe all the chords. I just sat in the basement and learned all the tunes and thought that these guys were really good. This was a long way from Bill Haley."*

DOUG MCKEEN (local music fan and entrepreneur): *"Most people don't know how ahead of the curve Ottawa was with The Beatles. Thanks to Sandy Gardiner, we had their records long before Toronto, Montreal or the States. Sandy would bring them back when he went to visit Britain and would offer them to Ottawa radio stations to play. So we heard them weeks and even months before other markets. We were ready for what happened.*

"I did perhaps the first North American Beatles book. When they appeared on Sullivan for the first time, a friend and I sat down in front of a television set and shot as many pictures as we could, and we had a Beatles book on the street within twenty-four hours. It was about thirty pages and all it was, was the pictures. We sold it all through the Valley and made a good bit of money on that one. I don't know if it was illegal. We just did it, and I've never seen a copy since."

CHUCK KERR (Octavian): *"I was eleven or twelve, so it's not like everybody in my circle was talking about it. I wasn't aware of them, but I couldn't believe what I was seeing. I was a school patroller, and the next morning I can remember one of the seniors at my corner on Maitland where I was working knowing all the words to The Beatles' melodies and singing the songs they had done. And the older kids were just talking about it and talking about it."*

The Beatles opened with "All My Loving," followed by the ballad "Till There Was You" from *The Music Man*, perhaps to show parents they really weren't so dangerous after all. The first set closed with "She Loves You," with the signature mop-top head shakes. The boys would return later to close the program with "I Saw Her Standing There" and "I Want to Hold Your Hand."

Legend has it that even if you had a black-and-white TV, your memories of that night are full colour.

Ed Sullivan and his wife had been at Heathrow Airport in London waiting for their plane home when they found Beatlemania or, to be fair, when Beatlemania found them! Entering the terminal, they were nearly run over by hordes of screaming girls. Turns out the kids were waiting for The Beatles to arrive home from a short tour of Sweden. Ed took a mental note. He had always regretted being late on Elvis. The King-to-be had already appeared on three network TV shows before Ed had booked him. He wasn't going to miss The Beatles.

It cost Sullivan $10,000 plus expenses to book the band, an unheard-of amount for an untested act. Brian Epstein was a tough negotiator, but Sullivan was no slouch either. While the deal ended up being $10,000 plus expenses, The Beatles had to tape enough material for two more shows. Ed won the short-term ad revenue battle, but Epstein won the long-term exposure war.

The moment Ed said good night with that signature wave, Beatlemania was in full throttle. The wigs, the lunchboxes, the magazines, the mugs, and…almost forgot…the records.

Every rock band in Ottawa started adding Beatles tunes to their repertoire. For The Staccatos, it was handy to have a manager like Sandy Gardiner, who was still very connected to the British music scene.

VERN CRAIG (THE STACCATOS): *"I think we were opening for The Beach Boys in Ottawa, and Sandy was able to procure a song called 'Eight*

Days a Week' about four weeks before its North American release. We learned the song and we played it opening that Beach Boys show. Everybody thought it was our song, and when The Beatles came out with it, they said 'wow.'"

Musicians wore what The Beatles wore, sang what they sang and hung on every article in the *Ottawa Journal*, *Citizen* or countless teen magazines that seemed to spring up overnight. If George was seen with a twelve-string guitar, there would be a run on Ottawa music stores the next day. If it said "Beatles," it sold.

As the pop star images dulled, the focus began to change to the actual music. As the Lennon and McCartney song-writing tandem peaked with *Revolver* and *Rubber Soul*, musicians began to concentrate more on the lyrical content of their songs, and even began writing material themselves. Those who didn't start to explore writing their own music would soon find themselves in real-world jobs.

And then came *Sgt. Pepper's Lonely Hearts Club Band*, the ultimate production-fest of sound and ideas. Now it was part of the artist's responsibility to work with a producer to turn record albums into works of art. Again, there was a natural culling of bands that couldn't keep ahead of the wave.

It's almost as if The Beatles were a small light fading off in the distance, tantalizingly just out of grasp for other musicians. And you'd better be on the ball if you wanted to keep up. By 1970, many of the followers had become leaders themselves.

THE BEATLES' OTTAWA CONNECTION

Although The Beatles collectively never came to Ottawa, this area did play a major role in their early success.

Well before famed U.S. DJ "Murray the K" started calling himself "The Fifth Beatle," Canadian DJs were playing the heck out of the early singles. "Love Me Do," "Twist and Shout" and "Please, Please Me" had already been hits in England by December 1962 but had not yet been released in North America.

Back in those days, the British Capitol Records office would send promotional copies of their newest releases to their regional offices. The regions could pick and choose what to release in their markets. The head of Arts and Repertoire for Canada, Paul White, liked this new band called The Beatles. His American counterpart didn't. So, Canada beat the U.S. to the punch on The Beatles with singles like "Love Me Do," "Twist and Shout" and "Please Please Me," and also on the long players.

It was White who cobbled together our first Beatles album, *Beatlemania! With the Beatles*, released November 25, 1963. The British release, titled *With the Beatles*, came out November 22, the day JFK was shot in Dallas. The U.S. version, *Meet the Beatles!* came out January 20, 1964. Yeah, I know. It's confusing.

Now let's blow the rest of your musical mind. Did you know why Smiths Falls is sometimes called "The Birthplace of Beatles Music in North America"? Of course, the Fabs never set foot in or near Smiths Falls, although Ottawa did put in a pitch to attract the band on their first tour.

Smiths Falls is where they pressed the millions of Beatles records that flooded the Canadian market in the wake of Beatlemania. Although the plant was owned by RCA Records, they made a deal to cut vinyl discs for Capitol Records.

According to Piers Hemmingsen in his fascinating book *The Beatles in Canada: The Origins of Beatlemania*, the factory "ran like a Swiss Watch" in those days, and was perfectly situated on the CN and CP rail lines, as well as major roads east and west for quick distribution. Its proximity to the U.S. border also offered up another opportunity, clandestine as it was.

The early days of Beatles record distribution in the States was spotty at best, with various small regional labels releasing the first singles with questionable quality standards. Serious fans and the more reputable retailers looked north and saw pristine Beatles records on a major label and licked their lips. But how to get them?

In the research for his book, Hemmingsen interviewed former employees of the Smiths Falls plant. One said, "There were literally railway cars at a siding in Smiths Falls that were, under cover of night, taking boxes and boxes of Beatles records across the border. I don't think stuff was happening that was recorded on the books." It was America playing catch-up with Canada when it came to the hottest band in the world.

I highly recommend Piers Hemmingsen's book. You can buy it at **http://thebeatlesincanada.com**.

THE ESQUIRES PT. 2

Don Norman was working with a folk band called The Claytons when he got the call.

One night when he returned from practice, he got the message that changed his life. "My mom said Gary Comeau called. I said, 'What?' I was so excited. So, I called him, and he said, in that cool way of his, 'I was just wondering if you'd like to join The Esquires?' I went to a secret rehearsal at Doug McKeen's house in the Glebe. I got the job doing mostly covers and a lot of material by Cliff Richard. Now I could do a bang-on cover of Cliff's vocals, so I was in."

It was all smiles and positivity till Don's enthusiasm spilled over. "One of the first questions I asked the boys was when I was going to get to meet their manager Sandy Gardiner. I was a huge fan of his column in the paper. And they went, 'Well, uh. You're not going to meet him.'"

The news that Sandy and The Esquires had parted ways had not yet reached the masses. "Thankfully, Capitol liked what they heard in the new demos and they kept us on. But I got the feeling that once Sandy left it was kind of like a ship without a rudder. We were just young kids and we really needed someone to guide us. With Sandy's direction I think the band would have gone a lot further than it did. That's just my opinion. It's unfortunate the way it went."

Despite the cloud of Gardiner's departure hanging over them, 1964 was a magical year for The Esquires. It was the year they dominated the local rock scene and stepped outside of the Ottawa market and became one of the top groups in the entire country. They became the first Canadian rock act to be signed by Capitol Records, where they released the first major label album by an Ottawa band. They were opening across the country for some of the biggest rock bands in the world, including The Rolling Stones, The Beach Boys and the Dave Clark Five.

The Esquires with the Dave Clark Five 1964

The Esquires opened for The Dave Clark Five and other major acts

The Esquires were also regarded as the best rehearsed and, as Gary Comeau brags, the best dressed band in town. "For the time we wore very, very expensive suits. We did a lot of instrumentals for dancing and when the British scene came along, more vocals. Our stage moves were very tight, and we had great harmonies. The guys singing were all good singers." They made other musicians jealous with their snazzy new Vox amps and professional look when they played Pineland every Thursday, Friday and Saturday. Like Richard, Gary says they could measure their success there by the parking situation. "We'd get there early and we couldn't find a place to park. Those were fun times. We'd play and play and play, and the kids would dance and dance and dance."

Original Esquires cover photo

Don Norman loved it. He was living his dream, even offstage. "We were at the Central Canada Exhibition in August of 1964 and we were going to be interviewed at the CFRA booth, which was in the Pure Food Building. They were playing cuts from our album while we were walking around checking out the midway. They had speakers everywhere just blasting out our music, and I was thinking, oh my God, that's me singing. It was so cool."

The hits kept on coming, some getting airplay across the country. "So Many Other Boys" was their biggest, and helped The Esquires win the first Red Leaf Award, a precursor of the Juno Awards, as Group of the Year in 1964. A fan in Winnipeg loved the band so much he called his group The Squires. His name was Neil Young.

Neil Young and The Squires

According to Gary Comeau, Neil comes back into our story in late 1965. "When I was with The Esquires, we were getting ready to play a gig and I got a phone call. 'Hi. This is Dewey Martin. I'm here with my buddy Neil from Winnipeg. We bought a hearse and we're on our way to California. We want a guitar player. Do you want to come and play with us?'" Gary turned them down.

Neil had played with a Toronto band called The Mynah Birds, fronted by future funk legend Rick James and featuring a real live talking mynah bird on stage. How could they not become stars? Might have happened, but it turned out Rick was up here dodging the draft, and when he was nabbed, The Mynah Birds' wings were clipped.

A few weeks later, Neil Mynah Bird bassist Bruce Palmer were stuck in traffic on Sunset Blvd. in the hearse, when Neil spotted Stephen Stills in the car beside them. He knew Stephen from some gigs they had done together in Toronto. They reconnected, and teaming with Ritchie Furay and former Jive Rocket Dewey started the enormously influential band The Buffalo Springfield.

In The Esquires camp, things couldn't have been better, or so it seemed. The Red Leaf Award, an album, more singles, airplay across the country, lots of gigs and great crowds. Gary recalls, "We were doing so well in our peak period,'64, '65, that we chartered our own airplane to go to recording sessions for our album so we could get back in time to play a gig that evening. We were actually making a small fortune for a bunch of young kids."

The Esquires had reached the top of the pops in Ottawa, but they were your classic example of a big fish in a small pond. Eventually that fish is doomed to suffocate. It was becoming clear that The Staccatos had taken the crown as Ottawa's #1 group. The times were changing, and The Esquires were more "yesterday" than "today."

Enter Brian Lewicki.

Brian Lewicki and The Esquires

Brian had wanted to be in a rock and roll band ever since he saw The Hi-Tones play a dance at Commerce High School in the late '50s. His first "band" was actually a two-piece combo with his neighbour and buddy Richie Patterson. "He lived right across the street from me and we grew up together. He had a little conga drum and I had a guitar, and we went to a dance at Fisher Park High School and did a couple of songs. That's the first time I ever played in front of people," Brian recalls. "Then we had a band called the Vibratones, which became The Barons. Bob Coulthart played drums. We were more a showband than a copy band."

The Barons

Despite their youth, The Barons caught on quickly with their slick stage show and tight musicianship. They landed a "house" gig at the Inter-Provincial Hotel, where they played five nights a week! Brian remembers, "We were fifteen or sixteen, and since we were underage, we'd play a set and then have to go sit out in the lobby. We thought it would make us look older if we wore jackets, so we bought these red jackets. Unfortunately, the waiters there wore red jackets too, so we'd always be asked to get people drinks. We'd go up north to Timmins and Sudbury and put on Beatle wigs for a set because they were just breaking big. We nearly got killed in a couple of places. It was pretty redneck up there. They'd grab you by the shirt and say 'play some f**king country.'"

Back in Ottawa, The Barons landed the plum gig of opening for Ronnie Hawkins and the Hawks for a two-nighter at the Oak Door. It was an eye-opener for Brian and The Barons. "When you see a band like that, it makes you want to work harder. We used to go down to the Esquire Show Bar in Montreal to see acts like Sam and Dave and the other major top R&B touring bands, and we worked that material into our act in The Barons. That's where I learned my thing. That's where I learned to be a frontman. You sell the band to the girls. Never mind the guys, the girls will bring them along. We later brought some of that influence into The Esquires."

With a lineup that included, over time, Doug Orr, Bobby Coulthart, John Martin, John Cassidy and Ted Gerow, it's no wonder Brian says, "Musically, The Barons was one of the best bands I was ever in."

The move to The Esquires began with the departure of Clint Hierlihy. He had reached that critical age when he had to choose between rock and roll and the real world of education and a regular paycheque. He chose the latter. His replacement was Brian Lewicki.

The offer to join The Esquires came from Richard Patterson with the support of then-manager Harvey Glatt. It seemed like a logical move to make. Lewicki could sing, play guitar and gave the band a stronger stage presence and more of a rock image He also had those deep ties with Richard. Brian Lewicki stepped in to play bass and do some singing.

Right off the bat, it was clear to Brian that there was a divide in the band. "I know it wasn't popular with some of the other guys, but the band was in a decline. I went because it was more money and an opportunity, so

I took it. The first show I did with The Esquires was opening for The Beach Boys at Maple Leaf Gardens. I was a bit nervous going from a high school gym to that."

The lineup didn't last long. Gary Comeau was the first to depart, and he made no secret of the reason why. "It's like any band with internal problems. Brian Lewicki came in on bass, and he started power-tripping. It changed the whole politics of the band and the complexion of the band musically. I wasn't happy with it, and the jobs we were getting weren't that great. There were a lot up north and all over the place. I was tired of travelling, so I just left the band."

Don Norman was the next to go. He started up his own band, Don Norman and the Other Four, with Gary Comeau. Soon, the old, cleancut look with the "very, very expensive suits" was dumped in favour of a more modern, casual appearance. The old set lists were thrown out, and the music became less pop and more rock and R&B. It was now Brian Lewicki's Esquires.

Another turning point came shortly after as The Esquires headed south to record in New York City. "The first songs I cut with the band were 'It's A Dirty Shame' and 'Love Hides a Multitude of Sins,'" says Brian. "'Dirty Shame' was written by Bill Hawkins of The Children with a folk style. Our producer said we should change it, so we rearranged it to have a more upbeat, rock sound, which worked much better for us. The song charted a bit down the east coast of the U.S. and we had an opportunity to go on these little mini-tours down in the States. But some guys didn't want to do it, so it was another missed opportunity. And I have to say I was a little upset about that."

And who was the party-pooper? "That was me!" admits Paul Huot. "I didn't feel like touring. I had a family and job commitments, so I had to take vacation time to do recording sessions and the short tours we would do. It really paid off when it was time to retire because I had a pension and none of my buddies did."

Paul's life as an Esquire was over, at least for now. By the time the next shakeup was done, no original members were left. High schooler Doug Orr was on bass, future Five Man Electrical Band member Ted Gerow was on keys, John Cassidy played guitar and Brian Lewicki was out front singing, playing some guitar and harp.

And this was not your father's Esquires. Gone were the sharp suits and nifty dance steps, replaced by casual mid-'60s rock fashions, a harder edge and a stage show that seemed lifted from the Esquire Show Bar in Montreal or the hottest clubs in the Kensington Market strip in Toronto. The band was red-hot and Lewicki was in his element as the master of ceremonies. "It's showbiz. They're paying you to entertain. That's the way we looked at it."

When Ted left for a better-paying job playing a full-time gig at the Glenlea Club in Hull, Brian pulled off a real coup by adding Bruce Cockburn of The Children to the lineup for a short time. Brian says, "Bruce taught us a lot. He taught me how to sing correctly. I think we all learned a lot from Bruce. Then he went off on his own to Toronto and the rest in history."

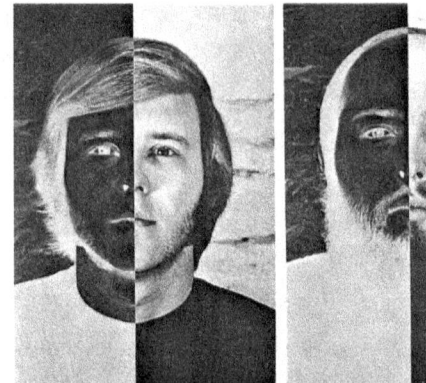

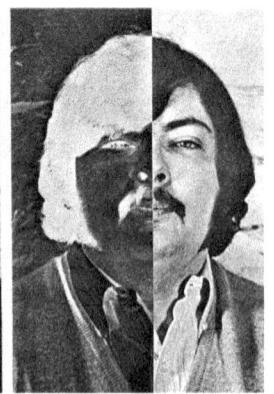

The Esquires Mach VI? Lewicki-Coulthart-Orr

Within a year The Esquires were history as well, although long-time fans might have said the band was over when Gary Comeau left. But all involved continued to contribute to the Ottawa scene. Gary joined Don's band Don Norman and the Other Four, and later reunited with Paul Huot in The Townsmen. Brian Lewicki, Doug Orr and Bob Coulthart would be the final lineup for the legendary MRQ. And after a brief attempt to put together the New Esquires with Paul and Gary, Richie Patterson would have great success with Canada Goose, which had a big hit with a cover of the Jackie Wilson tune "Higher and Higher."

Canada Goose

Still, it was sad to watch The Esquires fall apart like that near the end. But they had a marvellous run and set a high standard for other Ottawa bands nipping at their heels. They proved that an Ottawa band could make it on the national scene if all the right ingredients were in place. Who knows what might have happened if the Sandy Gardiner situation had been worked out?

Ironically, Gardiner's next project was to reach even higher levels in Canada and internationally. That band was to be The Staccatos.

THE STACCATOS: THE LONG WAY HOME

On a warm summer night in 1963, Vern Craig was doing what most red-blooded young men would do at the drive-in. He was writing songs. By the time James Bond has triumphed over the evil Dr. No, Vern had finished a song for his new band. The song was called "It Isn't Easy." His band was The Staccatos.

Normally rock bands evolve from relationships between friends, neighbours, or relatives. Members come on go and you kind of follow the flow till you make it or break up. Usually, it's a very organic process. It was a bit different for The Staccatos.

The band was a project put together by CKOY disc jockey Dean Hagopian. Dean had come to Ottawa from London, Ontario, in 1960. As his radio career at CKOY began to flourish, he decided to pursue another passion on the side. One was doing DJ duties at local dances. "I was doing dances at the Playhouse with Doug McKeen, and we needed a band to come in and play live. I chose a group called The Regals. I used them later to back me up on a single I recorded, which should not be mentioned too often," jokes Dean.

The Regals

With his dream of solo stardom fading, Dean decided it might be better to start up his own band that he would front. He started looking.

"I was in the Jive Rockets at the time," Vern Craig says. "We were playing with Hughie Scott at the Chamberland Hotel in Aylmer. Dean, at the time, wanted to start a band. He always had the thought that he wanted to front a band, so he said he had enough contacts that we could do okay. So we decided that we'd give it a shot. We got Brian Rading on bass, he came in from the Regals, and he knew a drummer named Rick (Bell) Belanger."

Originally Dean wanted to call the band The Stilettos. Vern hated the name, thinking it was the wrong image for a town like Ottawa. So, they came up with "Staccatos."

The original Staccatos with Dean Hagopian (middle)

"We played as the house band at the Oak Door on Bank," remembers Vern. "We would back up all the single performers who came in, like Brian Hyland and Gene Pitney. We were playing covers at the Green Door at the Chaudière on the Quebec side five nights a week, plus rehearsals. It was a tough club, but that's what really honed us a band."

The band was busy and starting to challenge The Esquires as Ottawa's top group. But Dean had hit a wall. "I had been at it for about a year and a half. I was pulling a radio shift from 4-8 p.m., then playing with the band four or five nights a week and socializing after the gigs—and I was a new dad. It was too much. It was killing me." Dean decided to pack up and move to Montreal, where he continued in radio.

In Vern's mind there was no thought of disbanding The Staccatos. The band was super tight and the gigs were plentiful. But without a solid frontman, it was all in jeopardy. Fixing this problem once again came at Hughie Scott's expense.

Les Emmerson had followed the usual musician's path in high school. He had played with several bands before he found his first success with The Profiles, who were good enough to open for the legendary Ronnie Hawkins at Pineland in 1963. Ronnie and the Hawks had a reputation as the hottest stage act in the country. The gig was an awakening for Les. "That was one of the most profound events of my life. I never knew live music could sound so good."

After a stint in Vern Craig's group the Jive Rockets, Les joined Hughie Scott's band. Hughie was the most exciting and seasoned stage performer in Ottawa in those days and the constant gigging quickly shaped Les into a showman as well as a tight musician. The country sounds weren't exactly his bag, but there were plenty of gigs and the money was good. But just when Les Emmerson seemed to have found his calling…

"Ladies and gentlemen, The Beatles. Let's bring them out."

The boys were playing on the Quebec side on that cold February night in 1964, but had timed their break so they could see The Beatles on *The Ed Sullivan Show*. Les calls it his "eureka" moment. "It was an earth-shattering moment for me, like when I first saw Elvis on TV. I knew at that moment I had to get into a band that was playing that stuff."

That night also had a huge impact on Vern. "We were babies then as far as The Staccatos were concerned. It was a fantastic sound, of course, and to emulate that is what people wanted. We were playing basically to make a living and trying to do something on our own, but we were there to make a living. That's what people wanted, they wanted to hear Beatles music and the British Invasion music. We were playing the Chaudière, and after we had records come out, we were playing universities, high schools, Pineland and everywhere else, and people wanted to hear that music. They wanted to be able to dance to it. And that's what we did."

The Staccatos' second home: the Chaudière Club Rose Room

Shortly after The Beatles hit, Les got a call from Vern asking him to join the band as their new singer. Les bid adieu to poor Hughie and joined The Staccatos, even though it meant a substantial pay cut. What sealed the deal was when Vern talked about recording original material. Les Emmerson was in.

"When I joined, they were just starting to add some original material to their shows," says Les. "Everybody was a cover band back in those days, and if you had original material, you kind of tucked the songs in between the cover hits. We did a lot of British Invasion material live, and even pronounced our words like the British did."

The first recording date for the classic lineup of the band was mid-January 1965. There were no truly professional recording studios in Ottawa at the time. Hy Bloom's place on Somerset at Bank was fine for doing demos, if you factored in stopping the tapes when the streetcars rumbled by, but for something that was playable on the radio, it was either Montreal or Buffalo. The Staccatos chose Buffalo.

It involved a long van ride, and Les remembers that trip very well. "We drove down to Buffalo in a snowstorm to record 'It Isn't Easy.' We had all our stuff in a U-Haul trailer, and it kept sliding. We looked out the window at one point and the trailer was even with the car and coming around. It was horrendous."

But the band made the trip count. The song they chose to focus on was the one Vern had written at the drive-in about a year and a half earlier. By April 1965, thanks to radio play and a big push from their manager Sandy Gardiner of the *Ottawa Journal*, "It Isn't Easy" beat out the latest Beatles offering, "Eight Days a Week," as the #1 song in Ottawa on the all-important Swing Set chart.

Bits & Pieces

THE SWING SET

A name that pops up frequently in this book is Doug McKeen. Doug wasn't a musician, but he left his mark on the Ottawa rock scene in the '60s.

He was a party DJ to start things off, which put him on the other side of the music scene in the eyes of most musicians. From that experience, he developed into the top sound guy in town, handling audio chores for huge acts like Cream, The Who and Jimi Hendrix when they came to Ottawa.

It was Doug who introduced a weekly publication that charted the sales and popularity of 45s in Ottawa. It was called *The Swing Set*, and no true music fan could walk by a stack of those foldouts in the record store without picking one up. That made Doug McKeen one of the most important music figures in town.

JH: So where did *The Swing Set* come from?

DM: The chart started when I met Sandy Gardiner. He was looking for a method to chart the hits, and really wanted it based on sales, to publish in the *Ottawa Journal*. I had the ulterior motive of getting free music from the record companies for my DJ work. Normally you would have to pay about $35 to get on their mailing lists, but I couldn't afford that. So we came up with *The Swing Set* that was published in the paper on the Youth Page and distributed as a one-pager in the record stores, Treble Clef, Sherman's Musicland, record bars in Perth, Smiths Falls, the Valley and down to Kingston. They had those wall shelves with slots for the 45s, and they would rearrange those every week according to what it said in *The Swing Set*. We phoned the record stores every Monday at noon to find out what their biggest sellers were, and that how we made the chart.

I would print them on Wednesday night, cut them on Thursday morning, go to school, then take them down to the post office in the afternoon. They would arrive at the stores Friday. We covered our cost with help from the record stores, the record companies, and local advertisers plugging upcoming shows at their venues. At best we broke even, but we were really doing this because of our love for the music.

JH: When did CFRA get involved?

DM: It was after about three years. The *Journal* had folded and the *Citizen* was the only game in town as far as print went. CFRA offered me a deal to continue to publish it but with the CFRA brand on it. So, it became the *CFRA Swing Set* and would feature photos of their DJs along with the chart and the ads.

JH: So was *The Swing Set* a legit chart, or was it doctored?

DM: Well, I contacted the record companies and told them if you give me free music, your songs will be tabulated, and I will give you the actual tabulation. If you don't give me the free records, you lose one point, which was basically a bribe. So that was the deal. It only took a #1 record to appear at #2 to convince the ones who didn't want to do it that they should do it.

The success of "It Isn't Easy" got the attention of Capitol Records, and by mid-year The Staccatos were on the same label as their idols The Beatles, The Beach Boys and The Esquires.

"It Isn't Easy" opened several doors for The Staccatos. They added a second drummer, Rick's brother Mike Bell (Belanger). There were more singles and more gigs, and by the end 1965 the band had transformed from a great cover band to a polished, professional concert group.

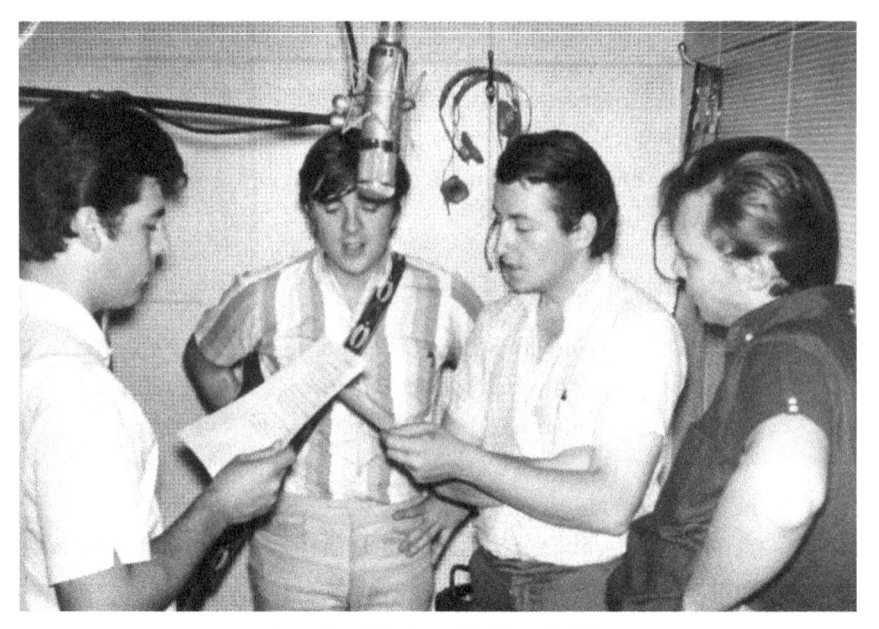

Recording "It's a Long Way Home," 1965

Sandy Gardiner was a key player in this evolution. He helped with the record label and worked with the band on their image and onstage presentation. And being Ottawa's most-read music writer didn't hurt either.

Although he was fair in his coverage of other bands, it became clear quite quickly that The Staccatos were now the top dogs in town. "In the beginning they were very much a jukebox band," Sandy recalls. "I kept saying to them that the only way you're going to break through the clutter is if you have some originality—what you can do that's different from other bands. We thought having two drummers and recording original material gave them that originality." Later, the Grateful Dead, Doobie Brothers and The Allman Brothers would pick up on the two-drummers format, but from my research The Staccatos were the first rock band to do this.

The Staccatos were also the highest-paid group in Ottawa. The band was pulling in a minimum $1,500 a show, which was a lot of money for those times. In today's money, that works out to over $12,000 a gig! For that, they could thank their super-agent, Lennie Leitch, professionally know as Leonard Alexander.

BITS & PIECES

SHOW ME THE MONEY!

Another important piece of the puzzle for the Ottawa rock scene in the 1960s was the emergence of the booking agencies. The most successful was the Leonard Alexander Agency, founded by Ottawa musician Lennie Leitch.

Lennie started playing drums while he was a student at Lisgar Collegiate, and went through the usual procession of pickup groups before he landed a job playing with the Billows brothers in The Hi-Tones, just in time to play on their debut album. The Hi-Tones were the top draw on the local rock and roll scene at that time and were landing some plum gigs around town. One highlight was an outdoor show at Lansdowne Park, where Lennie's career took an unexpected twist, literally.

The Hi-Tones were part of a bill that featured Johnny and the Hurricanes and an up-and-coming American singer named Chubby Checker, whose debut single was just starting to explode. That song was called "The Twist."

Originally recorded by Hank Ballard and the Midnighters in 1958, the song was redone by Chubby in 1960 and became a #1 hit around the world. Soon everybody from movie stars to grandmothers were doing the twist in the hottest nightclubs and dingiest basements.

Chubby's real name was Ernest Evans. It was *American Bandstand* host Dick Clark's wife who came up with his stage name based on another famous singer of the time. Instead of "Fats," she suggested "Chubby," and then went for "Checker" instead of "Domino." A legend was born.

Backstage at the Lansdowne show, Lennie asked Chubby how to do the dance. Checker went through the routine, and in no time Lennie had the basic moves mastered. They shook hands and that should have been just a cute story to tell the grandkids. But it turned into a lot more than that.

Shortly after that show, Lennie decided to strike out on his own as a solo singer. One night in Montreal, he wrangled his way on stage with a band and did his Twist shtick. The place went wild! Like the plot of a bad movie, a music promoter happened to be there and a star was born. Within days, Lennie had gigs lined up fronting a new band called Lennie and the Twisters, featuring guitarist Bob Hanni.

When the shelf-life of the group expired, Lennie and Bob came back to Ottawa and put together The Parkways with Wayne Tender and Carol Corbeau. They had a nice run and toured down to Toronto and down into the northern states.

The next career move for Lennie was much more adventurous. He hooked up with promoter Ron Scribner in Toronto, one of Ontario's biggest booking agents. With an eye on the untapped Ottawa market, Scribner worked out a deal with Lennie to expand into eastern Ontario. Ron would bring Toronto bands into Ottawa and Lennie would send Ottawa bands the other way. "The only problem with that," Lennie told me, "was that Ottawa didn't want Toronto bands. We were happy with the ones we had right here." From his threadbare one-room office on Bank Street, Lennie Leitch started booking Ottawa bands under the more refined handle "Leonard Alexander." He had the first rock and roll booking agency in Ottawa. "There were no agencies when I arrived. It was basically every band for themselves," he remembers. "I started salivating like a wolf. It was a golden opportunity."

It was also the biggest. At its height, the Leonard Alexander Agency was booking upwards of seventy bands, most of them two to three times a week. The Staccatos, The Esquires, The MRQ, The Townsmen, The Scoundrelz, Thee Group and many other top bands were kept busy making top dollars up and down the Valley, in arenas, high school gymnasiums and dance halls. There were so many places to play and so much money to be made that most Ottawa bands were happy just to stay here and not venture down to Toronto.

The rest of the decade was all milk and honey for Ottawa rock groups, but around 1970 things changed. I asked Lennie why the bottom fell out.

He told me, "It was simply this. The bands that were getting better known and drawing bigger crowds wanted to make more money. In a sense they out-priced themselves. At one point all the schools in the Ottawa Valley decided that this was crazy, they were spending way too much money. I think teachers found out how much money these bands were getting and said they were paying way too much for entertainment. So, they capped the amount they would pay. I think it was around $250. That just left the commercial operators to book bands, and there weren't enough of them to keep all the bands working. So the market dried up, just like this COVID thing."

As the clock rang in Canada's centennial year, all the elements were there for The Staccatos. They were tight, great songwriters, had great management, and amazing radio and print support. Best of all, they made excellent records. "I really loved the era around 1967-68," says Les. "We were voted the #1 band in Canada. We played for the Queen that year at Lansdowne Park. Every week we played at a place called 'Hidden Valley' in the Muskokas. We met and played with Neil Diamond, The Turtles, The Young Rascals, The Hollies and The Yardbirds. We would just watch and learn from those guys."

The only sour note for the band was the issue of airplay. I would put 45s like "It's a Long Way Home" and "Half Past Midnight" alongside anything from The Hollies, the Zombies or the other British Invasion bands of the time. But American radio ignored anything from north of the border, and there were no regulations yet in Canada to play The Ugly Ducklings, The Haunted and many, many other regional Canadian stars. This would change in a few years when Canadian radio was legislated to play homegrown talent, but there were few chances to make it big outside of your hometown before the Canadian Content Regulations in 1971.

The Staccatos would finally break through nationally in 1966 with "Let's Run Away," and then go Top 10 across the country in March 1967 with their brilliant "Half Past Midnight." But their biggest break came out of the blue in 1968, thanks to Coca-Cola.

BITS & PIECES

A WILD PAIR (1968)

How Jack Richardson pulled off *A Wild Pair* can best be described as a miracle.

In 1968, Jack was a long way away from being a world-renowned record producer with gold records like Alice Cooper's *Love it to Death*, Bob Seger's *Night Moves,* and a slew of Guess Who classics on his office wall.

He and three buddies had just started a new record label called Nimbus 9, with no money and no artists to get it rolling. Then came his "genius" moment. Richardson approached Coca-Cola with the idea of putting out a promotional record featuring Canada's two best bands.

The Staccatos had just won a Juno Award for "Let's Run Away," so they were a logical choice. And the Guess Who had scored a national hit with their cover version of "Shaking All Over," originally done by Johnny Kid and the Pirates. They had switched singers after that song, with Burton Cummings replacing Chad Allen, and they were now known across Canada thanks to their weekly involvement in CBC's *Let's Go*.

Somehow, Richardson secured the music publishing rights from Quality Records for the Guess Who and Capitol Records for The Staccatos. Coca-Cola gave the green light for the project, and the marketing campaign began.

To buy the record, you had to send ten bottle cap liners and a whopping $1 to a mailbox, and a few weeks later, there was your record. It sold around 85,000 copies, an astounding number at the time for a Canadian album, and pretty soon music fans from St. John's to Vancouver knew who The Staccatos were.

An interesting sidebar is that *A Wild Pair* was mixed by Phil Ramone, a young South African who would go on to produce stars like Dionne Warwick, Elton John, Stevie Wonder, Paul Simon, Frank Sinatra, Billy Joel and Aretha Franklin. I don't think you'll find *A Wild Pair* listed on his Wikipedia page.

The ball kept rolling for The Staccatos when Capitol Records U.S. caught wind of the success of the *Wild Pair* project. The Guess Who had been signed to Richardson's new Nimbus 9 label, but The Staccatos were already Capitol's. The company whisked the band down to L.A. to go for the big time.

The first chapter in the life of The Staccatos was now officially closed.

SOME "IDOL CHATTER" WITH LES EMMERSON

JH: How did you start playing music?

LE: I come from a very musical family, and there was always music in the house, so I grew up on music. I got a guitar for Christmas one year, an old Sears special, and it kind of sat behind the sofa for about a year. But when I saw Elvis on the Dorsey Brothers' show, I took that guitar and figured I had to learn to play it, 'cause I wanted some of that. There was no music like that up to that point, and right in my gut something happened and I had to play it.

All through high school I played. I had various bands under various names. We continually changed our name so we could continue to get work. The one band that was pretty successful was called The Profiles. We played with Del Shannon at the Oak Door when he came, and we opened for Ronnie Hawkins and the Hawks in 1962 at Pineland. That was a profound moment in my life that changed my life forever. I never knew live music could sound so good.

JH: You were playing in Hughie Scott's band the night The Beatles played Sullivan. What do you remember about that performance, and what effect did it have on the local music scene?

LE: When The Beatles arrived, the scene exploded. Before then, there were a few groups around, but not many. It was crazy after the Sullivan show. You would have three or four bands playing in one night in the church halls and teen clubs. The night they played I was gigging with Hughie Scott's band. We just took a break 'cause we had to see what all the fuss was about. And boy, that was another earth-shattering experience for me. I knew at that moment I had to get into a band that was playing that stuff, because they had new chords, new changes, new life. And the way they were dressed. I have no doubt that The Staccatos picked up on the Beatles style to always look good on stage. We had shirts and jackets and ties, which didn't last very long because it's not really comfortable to play live in suits.

JH: Tell us about your first professional recording session.

LE: We recorded our early material in Montreal at RCA Studios on Guy St. We got turned down by every label at first. Our first single, "It's a Long Way Home," finally came out on a small label called Allied Records. I had nothing to do with writing it but Vern put both our names on it because he wanted us to be a song-writing team like Lennon and McCartney. It was cool to have an actual writing team, but we very rarely wrote together. The single did well in Ottawa, which was enough to get us a label deal with Capitol.

JH: You were the house band at the Chaud. What was that experience like?

LE: The Green Room in the Chaud was like Madison Square Garden. That is why it was known as "The Snake Pit." We played in between the fights. It was horrendous to watch. I swore some guys were going to die with some of the fights that were there. It was always packed, and it was the most wonderful thing for us because we got to practice in front of a crowd. We found out what worked and what did not work night after night after night. And we'd try some of our original stuff out. It's very much like what The Beatles did in Hamburg. There is no substitute for getting up in front of a crowd and doing it. The crowd will let you know if it is not working, believe me.

Parkdale United Church was another great venue. It would be so packed you couldn't move. That was always fun to play in front of a crowd that big.

We were at gig in Smiths Falls one night and a fight broke out during the second song. The rent-a-cops jumped in and pretty soon we had about four hundred people fighting. The promoter paid us off and we left. On the way home we stopped at a hamburger place and this kid runs up to the van and pleads for a ride back to Ottawa. We said sure, and then we noticed he was wearing handcuffs. He had escaped from the police at our show.

JH: I still think "Half Past Midnight" is one of the best songs ever recorded in this country.

LE: Thanks. We recorded "Half Past Midnight" in Montreal at RCA Studios on four tracks. The recording of the strings on that song was one of the biggest thrills of my life. We were the first Ottawa band to have strings on a record. We had two violins, a viola and a cello. We recorded it and then double tracked it so it was actually eight strings. The clock sound was a woodblock. You hit it on top for the 'tick' and in the middle for the 'tock.' Sandy Gardiner banged on a Coke bottle, the guys were hitting tables and whatever else we could get out hands on to add to the sound. We were just sponges for learning new recording tricks and techniques. That is one reason we went down to Los Angeles: to record.

Welcome to the jungle, boys! The U.S. West Coast was not the land of surf, sun, and fun anymore. It was the land of sex, drugs and psychedelic rock and roll. It seems that the Jimi Hendrix prophesy, "You may never hear surf music again," had come true.

The Beach Boys were yesterday's news. Now it was The Doors, Jefferson Airplane, Grateful Dead, The Byrds etc. ruling the roost. It didn't take long to realize that The Staccatos just didn't fit in on many fronts. Hitting the restart button was the first order of business. The band name? Too old sounding, not hip enough. Gone! The slick wardrobe? Too 1965. Gone!

The new band name came from a song from their second album called "Five Man Electrical Band." Vern remembers it as, "One of those dear-to-our-hearts songs that tells a story of a band that always opens for the headliners, and they travel all night and go to the next gig. It told our story perfectly."

Next came "the look." The suits were left in the closet and in came hipper, more comfortable styles that fit in better on the Sunset Strip. The music got heavier but didn't lose that all-important commercial edge and rich harmony that Capitol saw as their bread and butter. All was in place for the Stacc…oops…Five Man Electrical Band to conquer America!

The Staccatos' "new look," 1968

It was also a chance for Les, especially, to spread his writing and studio wings. Recording and the importance of the album had taken a quantum leap forward in 1967 when The Beatles released *Sgt. Pepper's Lonely Hearts Club Band*. For Les, his first listen was a "jaw-dropping moment." He explains: "The day it came out, Brian and I listened to it at least five times in a row. I remember listening to it with my mouth hanging open, thinking how the hell did they do that? I know bands that quit! I knew people who said it was just lightyears ahead and they would never be able to do that, and they gave up. As for me, I just wanted to figure out how they did what they did in the studio. It took the recording studio to an art form."

What followed was a seemingly endless series of back-and-forth trips to Ottawa, and one final brilliant release under the name The Staccatos. "Half Past Midnight" won another Juno for the band in 1967, just as their L.A. experience was set to go. It is probably their best song as The Staccatos, and remains to this day Les' favourite song to play.

With all this wind in their sails, it came as a surprise when the band broke the news about the name change during a live interview on Gord

Atkinson's *Campus Club* show. Some questioned the wisdom of the move so soon after The Staccatos were named the #1 band in Canada.

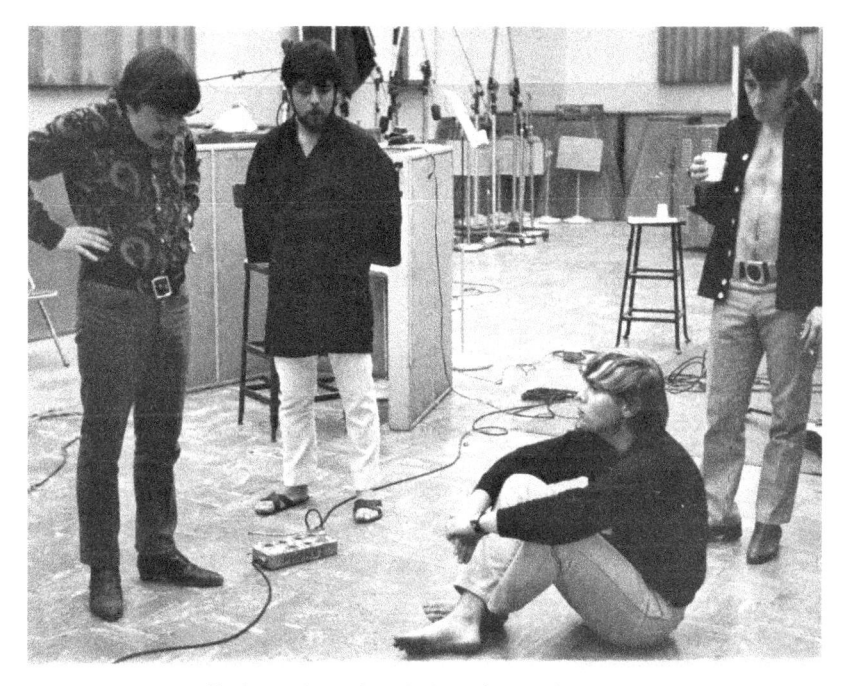

The boys relax and ponder life in Capitol's L.A. studio

It also came as shock to long-time fans when Vern Craig decided to leave the band to stay in Ottawa. One insider told me that Vern was not a fan of the California lifestyle, and preferred the slower pace of home. On his return to Ottawa, he went into band management and had success mentoring several local groups.

While no concrete explanation has ever been provided by the principal players, it is telling that the five songs chosen for *A Wild Pair* were all written by Les alone. The song-writing team of Craig-Emmerson was long dead by this time. The Five Man Electrical Band was clearly Les' band.

With changes made, the promotion train was running at full speed. The first order of business was to get that essential and elusive hit single!

THE FIVE MAN ELECTRICAL BAND RELEASES "SIGNS"

It was the kind of song that only comes around once in a lifetime for a band, if you're lucky.

"Signs" was recorded during the sessions for the Five Man Electrical Band's second album *Good-byes and Butterflies* in 1970.

> **LES EMMERSON:** *"We used to drive non-stop from Ottawa to L.A. to record till our money was gone, and then we'd come back and play and get enough to go back and try to get a decent record deal. And driving down through New Mexico and Arizona, it's like a western movie. You expect the Apaches to come over the hill, you know? I thought this is such magnificent scenery, but it's all getting covered over*

slowly with tourist signs. And people are spray-painting signs on the side of these gorgeous mesas. I just thought it was such a shame. That's where I got the idea for the chorus.

"*Then I got to thinking about all the negative things about signs always telling you to do something or you can't do something. I showed it to our producer when we got down to L.A. and he said, "You gotta finish this." It's great. So, I sat down, and I wanted to make the last verse positive. I thought of my religious grandmother and I wrote the verse about the church, that's a place where you're always welcome. And that's the story of "Signs."*

"*At first the song was released as the B side for "Hello Melinda Goodbye" in 1970, but it didn't get any airplay. So, our producer gave it to singer Bobby Vee, who was attempting a comeback. He had a moderate hit with the song in the States. Our producer persuaded our record company to re-release the song as an A side for us. So, if it wasn't for our producer Dallas Smith, "Signs" would never have been a hit.*"

Saying "hit" is a bit of an understatement. The latest figures say "Signs" has been played on the radio over one and a half million times and has sold over two million copies.

"Signs" remained the most successful single by an Ottawa artist until Alanis Morissette's *Jagged Little Pill* blew up in 1995 with hits like "You Oughta Know," "Hand in My Pocket" and "Ironic."

In 1990, the American hard rock band Tesla recorded a live, acoustic version of the song which was huge hit. It was on their album *Five Man Acoustical Band*, the title a tribute to the originators. Fatboy Slim also sampled "Signs" in one of his songs. The royalty cheques still make Les Emmerson smile!

Although sometimes called "one-hit wonders," the Five Man Electrical Band had moderate chart success with the follow-ups, "I'm a Stranger Here," "Absolutely Right" and "Werewolf," but the success arrow was slowly but surely tilting downwards. Still, "Signs" gave the band amazing airplay, some great opening and headlining gigs, and an appearance on *American Bandstand* in 1972. But by 1973 it was over. Les made some noise with a solo single called "Cry Your Eyes Out" in 1973, but that was about it.

Slowly the boys tired of the left coast and drifted back to Ottawa, regrouping from time to time for benefit shows and summer tours. These days, Vern Craig lives comfortably in British Columbia, and Les plays when he wants, still eying the mailbox for those royalty cheques. And they're still coming.

Back in that drive-in in 1963, Vern Craig must have dreamed what it would be like to be rock star. Les probably had those same dreams while he was choking on the smoke at the Chaud with Hughie Scott. They lived all the highs and lows, and The Staccatos stood on the peak just that one time. But they were there.

GLUED TO THE SET

We have talked a lot about the impact that radio had on the development of rock and roll in Ottawa, but let's not forget the good old "boob tube." Radio gave us the sounds, but it was television that put faces to the music.

In the States, the medium of television exploded after World War Two. The production of TV sets jumped from around 180,000 in 1947 to more than seven million by 1953 in the U.S. In Canada in 1947, there were just over 300 sets!

Just as well, since there was nothing to watch if you didn't live within spitting distance of the U.S. border and have an antenna. Here in Ottawa, the lucky ones could tune into grainy images out of northern New York State, but you had to either have the weather on your side or have some wacky, quasi-scientist neighbour who had a homemade TV antenna as tall as the CN Tower in his backyard.

Unofficially, Canadian broadcasting came to Ottawa on June 2, 1953, with coverage of the Coronation of Queen Elizabeth II, nearly live from London. In a feat that rivalled the building of the pyramids, videotape of the live broadcast in England was flown to Goose Bay, Newfoundland, via Royal Air Force bomber planes, then transferred to Royal Canadian Air Force fighters and jetted to Montreal, where it was broadcast to Montreal, Toronto and Ottawa a mere four hours after it happened live.

Regular TV programming started the next day in Ottawa, kicked off by a puppet show out of Toronto called *Uncle Chichimus and Hollyhock* at 6:45 p.m., wrapping up with pro wrestling at 9:30 p.m. The whole broadcast day was four hours, but CBOT was on the air on channel 4.

By the mid-'60s, cable TV was gaining steam, and we had access to many U.S. stations along with our own. We saw Elvis and The Beatles in black and white, but by 1966 TV was in glorious, living colour that would make a peacock envious.

Music was a huge part of programming back in those days, with variety shows presenting everything from opera, to show tunes to jazz and folk, and, yes, lots of rock and roll.

It took a while, though, for "our" music to get the spotlight it deserved.

Hootenanny was a show on ABC stateside that cashed in on the folk music boom of the early '60s. It ran just over a year and featured all the big stars of the genre, including The Brothers Four, Kingston Trio, The New Christy Minstrels and even our own homegrown stars Ian and Sylvia. The original host was New York radio personality Jean Shepherd, the writer and voice-over star of the classic *A Christmas Story* movie.

By 1964, the "folk revival" was on life support thanks to the British Invasion, so ABC cancelled the show and brought in veteran British TV producer and record producer Jack Good to put together the more contemporary *Shindig*, which featured the hottest rock acts from Britain and America.

NBC responded in January of '65 with *Hullabaloo*, with big-name guest hosts and the hottest charting artists of the day. The show featured weekly "drop-ins" from Beatles manager Brian Epstein in London, who introduced the latest British acts. In September 1966, with ratings sagging and music changing, *Hullabaloo* was replaced by another music series, *The Monkees*.

Shindig suffered pretty well the same fate. That same month, the show was "ka-powed!" in favour of a new show called *Batman*.

These shows are cool snapshots of the rock and roll boom of the mid-'60s, but the grand-pappy of them all had already been on air for a decade when they first aired.

It started as *Bandstand* on local Philadelphia TV in 1952, but when the eternally youthful Dick Clark took over the reins in 1956, it was re-titled *American Bandstand*. Kids would try out the latest dance moves, rate records and generally have a load of good, clean fun. The format was a winner, so it remained virtually untouched during its thirty-seven-year run. And since success breeds imitators, it didn't take long for most major U.S. and Canadian cities to try their own versions of *American Bandstand*. Toronto had *Music Hop*, hosted by Alex Trebek, which went on air in 1962. Halifax had *Frank's Bandstand*, and in 1961, another future media star would host Ottawa's version. It was called *Saturday Date*.

Peter Jennings, the first host of Saturday Date

Peter Jennings came from a broadcasting family. His father, Charles Jennings, was one of the big-hitters on CBC radio. After a variety of odd jobs and dead ends, Peter took the media plunge in 1961 when he was spotted by the newly arrived CJOH-TV. He reminded his boss of a young Dick Clark, so, in addition to his reporting duties, Peter was "volunteered" to host a new show called *Club 13*, which would soon be re-named *Saturday Date*.

Looking back at the few minutes of programming content that still exist, *Saturday Date* was basically *American Bandstand* on a budget. Up until 1966, the shows were in black and white, and the energy and dance skills in the room were not nearly up to par with the American cousin. Still, it was a kind of cool place to hang out at two o'clock on Saturday afternoons, and you got to know some of the regulars, like dance whiz Ricky "The Go-Go-Boy" Lefebvre. Many local bands were also featured miming to their songs during the show's eight-year run.

When Jennings was whisked off to the big time south of the border, CJET DJ John Pozer took over the microphone. In 1964, the honours went to DJ/singer Dick Maloney, who, like Gord Atkinson, was not a big fan of the music, leaning more towards the softer sounds of Frank Sinatra and Bing Crosby. Dick was the best showman of the bunch, and he handled the chore with class till *Saturday Date* went off the air in 1969.

There were other Canadian rock and roll options on the tube in that same time period. CTV had the nationally broadcast *A Go-Go 66* with Robbie Lane and the Disciples, which featured huge Toronto artists like The Paupers, Mandala, The Ugly Ducklings and a pre-Blood, Sweat and Tears singer David Clayton-Thomas. CTV dropped the "go-go" girls and re-branded the show as *It's Happening* in late 1966.

CBC had the biggest TV rock show hit when they combined several local shows into one cross-Canada series. They called it *Music Hop*, and later *Let's Go*. It was an after-school must for young rock fans, as the show travelled across the country with daily stops in Halifax, Montreal, Toronto, Winnipeg and Vancouver. Each episode would spotlight the talent in each of these areas, with occasional appearances or pre-taped interviews with major touring bands.

The most historically notable segment came from Winnipeg, where the "house band" was the Guess Who. Every Tuesday for two years, the band would cover hit songs of the day and do it with amazing skill. The band would also slip in the occasional original song. *Let's Go from Winnipeg* was a major reason the Guess Who broke through on a national scale and were chosen for *A Wild Pair* with The Staccatos.

THE TOWNSMEN

The revolution *was* televised.

It was revolution when Elvis sent the girls into ecstasy with a shake of his hips on *The Ed Sullivan Show*. It was revolution when The Beatles shook their mop-tops at the establishment who watched, amused, as their sons and daughters began their descent into moral hell. This was a revolution waged without pitchforks or red flags. It was a cultural revolution, and it changed the world.

In 1964, the coolest kid in the school halls wasn't the jock or the Head Boy. It was that nerdy kid from music class who grew his hair out a bit and carried around an armful of the latest records, or, better still, a guitar case. The posters of James Dean and Marlon Brando came down, and up went Mick Jagger and Ringo Starr.

On another hot, sweaty, magical Saturday night at Pineland in 1963, one of those kids, Frank Morrison, sat at one of the front tables sipping on his Coke checking out The Esquires…again. He watched how they moved, how they played the audience and structured their show to keep the kids dancing. And those amps! Brand new Vox amps, the best sound rig he'd ever seen. It was the envy of every aspiring musician in town.

The Esquires were the band Ottawa players admired and emulated in the early '60s. They were young but still thoroughly professional. They were headlining the best clubs, and played pretty well every church hall and school dance in the region. They even had records played on the radio and stories written about them in the newspapers! The Esquires were stars, and Frank Morrison wanted to be just like them.

Frank had come to Ottawa from the Maritimes as a child. His first band was an instrumental combo called The Ensembles. When needed, Frank would handle a vocal or two to add some variety to their shows.

He landed a "real" job at Statistics Canada and there met another musician named Wayne Leslie. Wayne's band was called The Darnells, and they were fairly well known around the club circuit. It didn't take long for Frank to work his way into that band.

The Darnells

The Darnells were a big step up from The Ensembles, with more gigs, better material and more chances to sing, which Frank loved. He was in

The Darnells that night at Pineland. He remembers watching The Esquires work the crowd, thinking, "Man. I would pay to play here." Little could he guess that The Esquires would play a major role in having that happen.

In 1966, The Esquires were beginning to self-destruct. They had had a great run, but it was obvious that changing times and directions were not sitting well with the band. When Paul Huot and Andy Legault quit the band, they decided to try something with more of a vocal approach. They were impressed with the tight harmonies of The Darnells and invited Frank, Wayne and David Milliken to jump ship and join their new band.

After about two months of solid "woodshedding," the as-yet-unnamed group debuted their new lineup with a house stint at the Coral Reef Club. They treated it as a showcase, playing Esquires material, jukebox hits and original material to old fans and anyone in the media they could drag out. And there was really only one guy they wanted in that front row. That was Sandy Gardiner. Finally, there he was.

Sandy was impressed with the whole package: the look, the material, the stage presence, and, especially, the vocal harmonies. It was something that Frank had worked hard at. "You had The Beach Boys, The Hollies, The Mamas and Papas, Paul Revere and The Raiders, all these bands had really heavy harmonies. That was the hot sound in Ottawa at the time, and one of the things we were noted for."

Gardiner and the guys came up with the name "The Townsmen" because it sounded classy and slightly British. Sandy added the band to his management stable, joining the red-hot Staccatos. The new relationship became obvious when The Townsmen played their first gig opening for The Staccatos at the Coliseum in front of more than 2,000 people. Then came the media campaign. The doors to the music industry were flung open because of Sandy's clout.

That clout brought immediate results. First was a deal with Regency Records. Next The Staccatos stepped in, with Vern and Les writing a song for The Townsmen called "I'm Such a Dreamer" for their first single. Sandy wrote about it, and CFRA, CKOY and CJET played the crap out of it. Tailor-made to take advantage of The Townmen's amazing vocals, it cracked the Top 20 in several Canadian cities and topped *The Swing Set* in Ottawa.

Frank will never forget the big moment of hearing the song on the radio for the first time. "We were in a car on the Queensway around ten after five. We had CFRA on, and the DJ said, 'Here's a brand-new band with a brand new song. It's The Townsmen with "I'm Such a Dreamer."' We were all screaming because we had never heard ourselves."

The Townsmen open the new Sparks Street Mall, 1967

The gigs started coming fast and furious for The Townsmen. Besides the clubs and basements, there were high-profile outdoor shows at the Ottawa Ex, during halftime at an Ottawa Rough Riders game, and even a free show on the Sparks Street Mall that drew thousand of kids.

With "I'm Such a Dreamer" riding high on the charts, The Townsmen embarked on their first cross-country tour, opening for touring American bands like Gary Lewis and the Playboys and The Young Rascals. Frank remembers that chaos and the frenzy of the fans. "I remember in Kingston we were mobbed by screaming girls and we ran to the dressing room and locked the door. We were all sitting there with big grins on our faces. We'd made it."

There was a different kind of frenzy in the air on March 1, 1967, at the Coliseum at Lansdowne Park. The Townsmen and The Eyes of Dawn were the opening acts for the legendary Animals from England. Once one of the top five British Invasion acts, the Animals were going through personnel and musical changes, as were so many other groups at the time. Fans were anxiously waiting to hear and see the results. But nobody was expecting what went down the night.

THE ANIMALS RIOT: MARCH 1, 1967

In 1966, the Animals were still a big name on the rock scene. In truth, the only true "Animal" left in the lineup was singer Eric Burdon. He and the "New Animals" were on their first North America tour, and the Ottawa Coliseum was one of two Canadian stops. Fan were expecting a special night, and they got it.

The Townsmen and the Eyes of Dawn opened the night with solid sets that were well received. Then the fans sat back to wait for the headliner. Little did they realize that backstage there was a very heated discussion going on between the promoter and the band's management.

There are various stories about what went down.

One story is that promoter Peter Charrier only wanted to pay the band $300 in advance, while the band demanded full payment of $3,500 before they played a note. Charrier wouldn't budge, so the band walked.

Another says the two parties could not agree on set lengths. Eric Burdon and the New Animals had been contracted to play two 40-minute sets, but they wanted to do only one 50-minute set. Charrier agreed but wanted to play the band less.

Whatever the fine points were, it didn't really matter to the crowd, as the fidgeting, hand clapping and cries of, "We want the Animals!" started. CFRA DJ Al "Pussycat" Pascal was hosting the evening and was doing his best to maintain some sense of calm. Something was obviously wrong. After nearly an hour and half of this, the positive vibes of the earlier evening had evaporated, and the kettle boiled over.

Doug McKeen was near the front of the house in his usual spot behind the soundboard. As Ottawa's top soundman, he did all the big shows, including Jimi Hendrix and The Who. But this was different. Something just wasn't right.

There were three things that concerned him. First off, this break between acts was just way too long, and there was not even a guitar on the stage. Number two, the promoter was gone. Rumours that he had fled to Jamaica were never proven. The worst warning sign was that Eric and the Animals had left and gone home. No guitars, no promoter, no band, and, likely, no show.

This was going to get ugly real fast, and the only thing lying between an increasingly belligerent crowd of 2,500 kids and a stage full of expensive sound equipment were Doug and his crew of four. But Doug had a plan, and it wasn't found in the soundman's handbook.

DOUG MCKEEN (SOUND ENGINEER): *"We had our sound system up on the stage, but I knew if we started moving the equipment off the stage, everybody would know there wasn't going to be an Animals show and there's going to be some problem. I had about four guys with me, so I sent them out into the audience to grab whoever the hell they knew, brought them back to the side of the stage. We made everyone responsible for a given item on the stage and told them to get up there, grab it and get the hell off the stage and into the truck as quickly as possible. So we made our move, the crowd figured out what was going on, and in two minutes the entire stage was flattened and there was a fire happening in front of the Coliseum. It was scary, but being young and stupid, we sat in the top row watching it happen. Every chair was broken, the panels on the hockey boards were flattened. It was just a just pile of boards on the ground."*

Al "Pussycat" Pascal had a different perspective on the goings-on that night. He had been hired to be one of the MCs for the show and was right in the line of fire when things went bad.

> **AL PASCAL (CFRA DJ AND HOST):** *"Dean Hagopian, John Pozer and I were all hosting that night, taking turns on stage. The crowd was getting rambunctious to put it mildly. We just tried to delay and delay by saying Eric and the band will be out soon, but I could see nobody was setting anything up, and Eric was sitting in the back. They were throwing chairs on stage. So we went into the referee's booth to make announcements because it was covered like a little shack. Finally I went into the back to talk to Eric. I did it a couple of times. We were just in a dressing room sitting on a player's bench. I said, 'Eric you've got to get there.' And he said, 'If I don't get my f***king money in fifteen minutes, I'm f***king out of here.' He just kept repeating that. So, after the fifteen minutes, he was gone. The promoter, Peter Charrier, declared bankruptcy, so I didn't get paid either. I was told later it was the first time the Riot Act was ever read in Ottawa."*

As you can imagine, the newspapers had a field day, with stories about "juvenile delinquents" and the "dangers of rock and roll." The headline in the *Ottawa Journal* read "Youth Running Wild!"

Thankfully, there were no injuries, just a few arrests and not many charges laid. Damage was pegged at around $8,000. Really the only big repercussion was that there was never another rock and roll concert at the Coliseum.

Days later, the group issued a written statement on the event. "Eric Burdon and the Animals express their sincere regrets to all their fans in Ottawa, Canada. The non-performance at the Coliseum last Wednesday night was occasioned by no fault of Eric or the group, and was attributable solely to the promoter. Eric has expressed his desire to return to Ottawa as soon as is reasonably possible to entertain and perform for all his fans."

Eric kept his word. He returned to play at the Palais des Congrès in Hull in 1983. I guess he had a very busy schedule.

Luckily for The Townsmen, and their equipment, they had left the concert right after their set, so the Animals "riot" was just another memory of an amazing year.

Shortly after the Animals show, there was a major shakeup in the band, which resulted in Gary Comeau, the driving force behind The Esquires, joining on guitar. Gary has always loved The Townsmen's emphasis on vocal harmony, and that was front and centre for what would be their signature tune.

"The Lion Sleeps Tonight" had been around in one form or another since the 1920s. The American vocal band The Tokens had a fair-sized hit with it in 1961. With its soaring harmony parts, "The Lion Sleeps Tonight" was right in The Townsmen's wheelhouse. It jumped off the radio and into the Top 30 nationally. Recorded on the Regency label, "The Lion Sleeps Tonight" was the second Townsmen song to top *The Swing Set* chart in 1967.

"We're Doing Fine" and "He's In Town" kept up the momentum, but by 1968 the ride was ending for The Townsmen. The singles stopped charting, and then Gary Comeau and founding member Wayne Leslie split to pursue new projects. Wayne hooked up with singer James Leroy and Gary reunited with Richard Patterson and Paul Huot in Canada Goose.

James Leroy and Denim

Like The Esquires and The Staccatos, The Townsmen made it to the top of the Ottawa music scene thanks to their professionalism, strong vocals, radio and press support, and the steady guidance of Sandy Gardiner. All three bands landed major record deals, toured the country, and had chart success in major markets from coast to coast.

There was also a healthy competition between the three, which made them all better. It's also interesting to note the inbreeding and sharing of material that took place. The Staccatos wrote a couple of hits for The Townsmen. The Townsmen toured as openers for The Staccatos. Gary Comeau played guitar with all three bands. If The Esquires had a small tour van, the other bands would buy vans too. If one band had a roadie, another would have two. All three wanted to be top dog but they would support their rivals and cheer for them to make it as well.

There was no competition for gigs because there were so many places to play. Frank Morrison did a count once and found that in 1966, "there were sixty-seven local bands and they were all working, in places like The Tower, Riverside Gardens, Pineland, church basements, all over the place. It was a golden situation for local bands. They were making good money, making records, and back then that was a big deal."

From 1965-68, there was little doubt who the top three bands in Ottawa were. The Staccatos had wrested the crown from The Esquires, but they were still a close #1 and #2. Thanks to an impressive run of hits, The Townsmen were just behind.

But there was room for another contender for the crown of Ottawa's best band. The fourth face on our "Mount Rushmore of Ottawa Rock" in that period, was possibly Ottawa's coolest band.

DON NORMAN AND THE OTHER FOUR

Every musician knows what it's like to be summoned to a "band meeting." It is the music equivalent of "the boss wants to see you in her office" or being sent to the principal's office. You know something bad is going to happen.

Don Norman wasn't surprised when he was called in. The last few months had been rough for The Esquires. Long-time members Gary Comeau and Clint Hierlihy had left, not pleased with the new musical direction of the band they had founded. Brian Lewicki was the de-facto leader of The Esquires now, and he was pushing to change their sound and image to better fit in with the changing times.

"It was unfortunate the way I left the band," Don remembers. "The music was changing. The Beatles started out looking like The Esquires with their suits, but once they dropped that and started dressing as individuals, and the Stones came along looking kind of rough, the image of rock bands really changed a lot. I was kind of the pretty boy who sang out front to the girls. I was more in the mould of a Cliff Richard or Bobby Vee. Brian had already been a guitarist and lead singer in his previous band. I think the other guys were thinking I was a little dated here and if we don't get with the times, we're going to get left behind. At the meeting they just spelled it out to me. It really hurt, and I got angry and stormed out. It was not a happy ending."

In younger, happier times, twelve-year-old Don Norman was probably one of Ottawa's top "hairbrush singers." In 1957, his bedroom fantasy took a major leap into the real world when Elvis burst on the scene. Although his mom wouldn't let Don attend the Presley concert in Ottawa the next year, she made up for it. After seeing his latest movie *King Creole*, Don remembers, "She was so impressed she marched up Sparks Street to Orme's Furniture, bought a flat top guitar, came home, said, 'Here take this.' I haven't put it down since."

With the help of his lifelong friend Dave Milliken, Don learned some basic chords. Within a year, he was writing songs inspired by his idols: Elvis, Buddy Holly and Chuck Berry. He remembers his first gig as a house party, where he played and sang with Dave and their friend Bruce Cockburn.

Then came his first groups: The Continentals in 1961, who recorded a song at the famed Hy Bloom Studio on Gladstone; then came The Jades, who "actually played Pineland, and got paid!"

The big break came when he joined Ottawa's top band, The Esquires, in 1963 just in time to start recording the band's first album on Capitol Records. The skinny kid with the hairbrush was now fronting Ottawa's biggest rock band.

Then came the big gigs, the records, the tours, the adulation. And finally came "the meeting."

Hell hath no fury like a fired lead singer. The day after his sacking, still hot, Don went down to the local Patents Office and bought the name "The Esquires."

"The deal at the time was that I would stay in the band to fulfill our obligations until Brian was ready to take over singing. Later that week, Paul Huot called me and asked if I was coming down to Cornwall that weekend to play a gig. I said 'I don't think so.' There was a pause and then

Paul said, 'You're lucky. We would have beat the sh** out of you!' I guess you could say there was some bad blood between us."

Still disillusioned with the way the whole situation had gone down, Don quit music for a short time and took a job as a taxi driver. A chance meeting one night downtown with his old friend Gary Comeau reeled him back in. "We grab dinner and Gary says, in his cool way, 'So I got a new band going. It might not go anywhere. You interested?' With an offer like that who wouldn't be?"

Don broke out the old hairbrush again to do some practising, and soon they were gigging around town as Don Norman and the New Esquires. Meanwhile the original Esquires were still playing, so obviously something had to give. There were threats of lawsuits, which would be costly and hold back both bands for years, so Don finally relented and gave the name back to the original Esquires. Their new band name came from Gary Comeau and was a bit of a swipe at their old mates. They were now "Don Norman and the Other Four."

Don Norman and the Other Four

Don Norman and the Other Four had also lined up some high-powered help in the person of local DJ John Pozer. Pozer was instrumental in getting the band a deal with Quality Records, and later co-founded a local label called Sir John A. with Ron Greene of the Other Four, in large part to push Don's abilities as a songwriter and to improve on the weak publicity provided by Quality Records for their first singles. It was a smart move, as the first release was "Low Man" in November 1966, probably the band's best release.

Pozer also persuaded the guys to steer away from the pop covers and go for something grittier and harder, like what the Paul Butterfield Band was doing. It was the first time Ottawa rock music really developed an "edge."

Don Norman and the Other Four were a solid commercial success in the Ottawa area, selling records and getting good play on local radio stations. Though they never really broke out nationally like The Esquires and The Staccatos, their singles "Low Man," "The Bounce" and the Dylanesque "All of My Life" remain classics of the '60s Ottawa scene, and fetch big bucks in record-buying circles on the web. "I've heard us described as Ottawa's most underrated band, and I think it's kind of true," says Don. "We weren't as polished as The Staccatos. Those guys were so good, total professionals, so they were on a different level. They were full-time musicians, playing six or seven nights a week. They were like The Beatles playing over in Hamburg, playing to get better."

Musically speaking, Don Norman and the Other Four were pretty heavy by Ottawa standards. They didn't go for the intricate harmonies of The Staccatos or The Townsmen, or the instrumental tightness of The Esquires. Don remembers the Other Four as, 'A hard-rockin' band, much harder than The Esquires had been. We did tunes by Mitch Ryder and the Detroit Wheels, Question Mark and the Mysterians, Wilson Pickett, that kind of stuff." Throw in a touch of early garage-rock and you have a band more along the line of the Stones than The Beatles or Beach Boys. That's why their music still sounds fresh almost sixty years later.

It was the departure of restless Gary Comeau that started a long death spiral for the band. This time Gary was off to join the harmony-rich Townsmen with his old friend Paul Huot. It was a real hard blow for Don. "When Gary left the band to join The Townsmen, that was a heartbreaker. It was devastating. The band was never the same after that."

That is an understatement. By the end of 1966, Don and John Pozer decided the best thing to do was to basically start from scratch, with new players and a new musical direction. Ron Greene and Don were the only members of the original band who stayed on, while members of the Ottawa band Bittersweet were brought in to fill out the roster. The blues and harder rock material was dumped in favour of a new, more pop-oriented sound. Out went the Mitch Ryder and R&B tunes and in came the Monkees and Gary Puckett. At first, the guys in the band took a "grin and bear it" approach to the new repertoire. But when they saw the kids, and especially the girls, all up dancing and having fun, they softened up and had fun themselves.

Don Norman recording at RCA Studios, 1966

The "new" Don Norman and the Other Four didn't last long. By the end of 1967 John Pozer had moved to Toronto to work in the music business, and Don decided to pack it in. He was tired of the touring and the pressures of running a rock band. His dismissal from The Esquires weighed heavily on Don till he retired. There was also a sad feeling that what he had experienced in those early days was gone forever and would never be back. "It was so different in those days. They had teen dances everywhere.

I don't think we ever played anywhere where they were drinking. The kids were sober and just having fun. And there were so many places to play: church basements, sock hops, school dances and clubs. Those were different times, and it will never be like that again."

Don Norman retired from active playing at the ripe age of 23. I can still see him grinning as he walked around the Ottawa Ex in the summer of 1964, hand-in-hand with his girlfriend, listening to his band blasting from the speakers. That is called living the rock and roll dream.

THE BOSS SOUNDS

John Pozer CJET Radio

For every music fan growing up in the 1960s, the best way to connect with the music of the day was through your radio speakers. Portable record players were just starting to work their way into kids' bedrooms, and music-themed TV shows were still very much an American phenomenon.

I would wake up to "General" Grant on the CFRA morning show, ordering us off to school with a hearty "Forward Hooooo!".

After supper, it was upstairs to do homework, which was more about keeping track of the hottest new songs than memorizing provincial capitals. I was a card-carrying member of Gord Atkinson's *Campus Club*, but that didn't stop me from skimming down the dial to hear what Nelson Davis was playing on CKOY. Then it was back to Gord, or that new wildman Al "Pussycat" Pascal.

And then there was that magic night when Gord Atkinson himself read my name on the radio for sending in a letter to the *Campus Club*. I won a whole case of Coca-Cola, but bigger still, the next day I was the coolest kid at Rideau High School for the first, and only, time.

I never dreamed of being a rock and roll disc jockey like these guys. They were on a level that was unattainable to a common kid like me. Prime Minister? Maybe. DJ? Never.

Just to take you behind the curtain for a moment, I've found there are two kinds of people who find their way onto the radio dial.

The first group work for it. They go to broadcasting schools or places like Algonquin College to learn the ropes. On graduation, it's usually a few years in a small market doing odd jobs, and then, if the gods are on your side, someone doesn't show up for their on-air shift and you are the only one around who knows how to turn on a microphone. Then a few more years of sending out airchecks to big-city program directors, and then, if the radio gods forget that they already gave you a break, you get a job in a major market, where you are overworked and underpaid. But, they'll tell you, it's show business! Be thankful for what you have.

I was in group #2. I was at Carleton University in the journalism program when I heard about this cool radio station they had called CKCU. This is before the station was granted an FM licence in 1975 and became Ottawa's first rock/jazz/blues and everything else radio station. How a group of scruffy young hippies managed to get on the air and stay there, and make great radio to boot, was a miracle.

I put in a call in the summer of 1973 and asked for a shift, not necessarily to be a DJ, but because I really loved music. I kept pestering them, and pestering them, and eventually I found myself standing in front of two turntables and a complicated sound board with a stack of vinyl, trying to figure out what to do. I guess I pushed the right buttons. The speakers were up high, my headphones were on "bleed," and I didn't sit down for the full hour. A year and a half later, I was doing two prime-time shows in stereo for the entire city, and I could play whatever I wanted! Ironically, nearly fifty years later, I am doing the same thing on LIVE88.5 with my show *The Sound of the Underground* on Sunday nights. No playlist, no boundaries. I still do it standing up, and the headphones are still on "bleed."

But, enough about me. Let's get back to those "wild west" days of the 1960s Ottawa radio.

One of the most memorable movie scenes of the '60s happens near the end of Sergio Leone's spaghetti western *The Good, The Bad and the Ugly*. The big finale is set in a graveyard, with the three protagonists facing off in a classic showdown. The camera lingers on each gunfighter, hands at the ready, eyes darting back and forth to read the others' thoughts. It's a standoff that only one man will walk away from, but who will it be? Who will blink first?

Drop the six-shooters and the ponchos and you've got the Ottawa rock radio war of the mid-'60s. Three men, armed with the hottest 45s, facing off every weeknight for the lucrative Ottawa teen radio audience.

First off the draw was John Pozer, first because his shift went from 4:30 to 7 p.m. weekdays on CJET radio in Smiths Falls, just outside Ottawa. At 7 p.m., it was the clash of the titans, with Nelson Davis and his *Teen Beat Show* on CKOY, and down the dial at CFRA, Al "Pussycat" Pascal. While Pozer had the audience all to himself with the after-school show, Davis and Pascal had teens jumping up and down the dial, playing basically the same music, but always looking for that "exclusive" song the other guy didn't have. If that meant hooking up a tape machine to record some station in New York State, that was fair game. A few swipes with the editing blade and you had your "exclusive," albeit usually not of the highest sound quality. It was a technique all three would use, looking for that little edge over his competitors.

This radio war was both cutthroat and friendly. Pozer, Davis and Pascal were respectful of each other, and it wasn't unknown for them to share songs with the others for a similar favour down the road. It was also ideal for the ever-growing army of young music fans who were looking for both the biggest hits and the newest singles while they pretended to do their homework in the bedroom.

My favourite time was late at night under the covers with my "Rocket Radio," so named because it was shaped like a rocket ship with the antenna coming out the nose. Plug the wax-encrusted earplug in and you had a ticket to Al Pascal's *The Final Hour*, which featured deeper album tracks and the coolest psychedelic sounds of the day. The music was changing, and radio was changing with it.

SOME "IDOL CHATTER" WITH GORD ATKINSON

Gord Atkinson and another guy

It's ironic that the man who brought rock and roll to Ottawa radio was not really a fan of the music.

Even when he was the #1 rock DJ in town spinning the freshest new tunes for teens on CFRA, Gord Atkinson admits he was a little "long in the tooth." But we didn't know, because he was on the radio and we idolized him.

After starting radio in Toronto, Gord came to Ottawa to work at CFRA in 1954. By the time he hosted Elvis Presley on stage at the Auditorium, Gord had already been in the radio business for a decade and he had just hit the dreaded thirty-year plateau. His list of friends and acquaintances included Golden-Age movie stars and singers like James Stewart, Bing Crosby, Bob Hope and his old Ottawa buddy Rich Little. He was very much an odd standard-bearer for rock and roll. But that was the position he found himself in when the music began to make waves in the late '50s.

JH: What did you think of the rock and roll movement when it started in the '50s?

GA: When rock came along, I thought it would be like another folk era. I never dreamed it would have the staying power that it did, and that it would take over popular music. People sometimes say to me, you were the first person to play and introduce Bill Haley, and Presley and all the other recording artists who came along. Then the British Invasion with The Beatles, Herman's Hermits and all those people. And I say quickly, listen. I'm no futurist. I had no idea this music would have such lasting power.

JH: How did you become the guy to bring rock and roll to Ottawa radio?

GA: The folk movement was so predominant at the time with The Kingston Trio, the New Christy Minstrels and The Brothers Four. That's really all you heard on radio as far as pop music goes. Rock and roll was a foreign sound to older ears, and I personally had a hard time on CFRA playing a lot of this music. I finally convinced the powers that be to take one block of time and just play music the younger generation wanted to hear. My boss Frank Ryan [the "FR" in CFRA], said okay, let's try one show and see how it goes. So, we rented time at the Coliseum at Lansdowne Park and we put on this first CFRA Campus Hop. I just prayed that someone would show up because my reputation was on the line. We had hundreds and hundreds of kids that lined up. We had about 3,000 kids packed into the room. From that success we began the radio show *The Campus Corner*, which ran from four to six Saturday afternoon. We started a club atmosphere and then Coca-Cola jumped on board as our sponsor. They came up with the name *The Coca-Cola Campus Club*. We would do the show live from the Ex for years, and we would get thousands of kids down for them.

JH: As the top jock in town, you got to introduce and meet Elvis in 1957. What do you remember about the show?

GA: In those days, our old radio studio was on the second floor of the Auditorium. As soon as I walked out on that stage, the kids knew that Elvis was going to follow me. The screaming of the crowd was so overwhelming, you couldn't even think. I opened my mouth to do this well-thought-out introduction for this fellow and nobody heard a word I said. I have no idea what he sounded like! The noise level was so high I'm surprised the roof didn't come off the place. The only time I heard a louder crowd reaction was when Dick Maloney, Max Keeping, who was working a CFRA at the time, and I were flown down to Toronto to Maple Leaf Gardens to see The Beatles.

SOME "IDOL CHATTER" WITH AL "PUSSYCAT" PASCAL

"Pussycat"

The CFRA Swingset
DIAL 580
Box 4054, Stn. 'E' Ottawa 1, Ont.
CFRA SWING SET FOR FRI. JAN. 26, 1968

THE FINAL HOUR....
.... IT'S A GAS!

THE CFRA-SWING SET
published weekly by
Canadian Music News — 235-6830

When he was a kid growing up in Montreal, Alexandre Pascal would sneak a rather bulky tube radio into his school classes so he could listen to Montreal Royals baseball games. He carried that passion into his late teens and early twenties with a string of radio jobs from Amherst, Nova Scotia, to Dauphin, Manitoba, and then back to Montreal, where he worked at a multilingual station. A cool job turned into a career when he landed a spot at CFRA in Ottawa in October 1965.

His timing was perfect. Gord Atkinson's "Coca-Cola Club" was hot, and the station was looking to expand their rock and roll reach into the later hours.

When Al started, Gord was on 7 to 8 p.m., Al took over the pop music from 8 to 9 p.m., then he changed hats, literally, and spun country music using the name Al "Tex" Pascal, then rounded out his shift with light, romantic music from 10 to 11 p.m. In time, management was persuaded to go all hits in that slot, and the legend of Al "Pussycat" Pascal began.

Al brought a different style of radio to Ottawa. It was more based on the American DJ style, with fast patter, crazy characters, production bits and an in-your-face barrage of news, jokes and music designed to keep you from flipping down the dial to see what Nelson Davis was playing on CKOY.

> **JH:** Where did your famous "Pussycat" nickname come from?

> **AP:** It actually came from a Brylcreem hair product commercial on WABC Radio in New York. In the middle of it, there was a really sexy voice that said "Hi, Al pussycat." Well, that's me, I guess. Guess I'll snap that one up and fit it into the show. So I brought my producer's girlfriend into the studio after hours and she recorded a series of voice promos like that. You just milk that kind of thing and have a lot of fun.

> **JH:** I have heard rumours that you and some of the other DJs were big fans of American radio content.

AP: Our engineer was also a ham radio operator. He used to record airchecks on American stations. I heard this one tape of Cousin Brucie on WABC New York, and one of the songs that stood out was "Hey Jude" by The Beatles. Now it hadn't been released yet in North America, but Cousin Brucie, being the most important DJ in New York, got an advance copy and was playing it. So, I made a copy of the tape and started playing "Hey Jude" on CFRA. Then we started getting complaints from the other stations in town, wondering why we had it and they didn't. So we got a cease and desist notice saying don't play it, it's not released, where did you get it—it was a big deal. I asked my boss if I was in trouble and he said, "Well, maybe I haven't received the letter yet…wink, wink." We played the heck out of it for the next few days. So, I got away with that and several other songs too. I used to write to jingle companies in the States and ask for samples of their rock station IDs. I would edit the ones that fit and use them on my show. The other stations were wondering how I could afford these jingle packages, and they sounded great. CHUM headquarters wondered why we didn't use the jingle packages they put together for their other stations, but I said they just don't fit over here. So they backed off and let us do our thing, because we were successful. That's what made the sound more Americanized, with more excitement. It was beg, borrow or steal to get one foot up on the competition.

JH: In those days, CFRA had a reputation as being a locally owned "Ottawa Valley" radio station, with a distinct Ottawa sound. How did that heritage survive when you were bought out by CHUM, which was a big chain run out of Toronto?

AP: When CHUM bought us in 1967, they tried to take over, like any station they took into their fold. They telexed the program director at CFRA and said, "Here are the songs that CHUM is playing in Toronto, and here's a list of songs you're playing. Please delete those songs and replace them with the songs we're playing." There was a lot of R&B and soul music, which was huge in Toronto. I told our program director that that music doesn't make it here. We have our own market, and we have our ears to the ground and know what our listeners want.

Needless to say, there were a lot of complaints from CHUM. But Terry Keilty, our boss, said "Listen, you own us, but keep your distance. We'll run it like a successful business. We need our space. We are not CHUM #2. We are successful at what we do." But he told us, "Keep in mind, if the day comes we go down in the ratings, the steam-shovel is going to come in." And that eventually happened.

JH: Were the DJs of that era allowed to play basically whatever they liked?

AP: A lot of stations had very tight rules about music programming back then, like never play female artists back to back, or never play two groups in a row. At CFRA it a was kind of gradual evolution towards more freedom for us to do creative things. You'd watch your step and you go ahead and do it. You would push the envelope and pay the consequences if it didn't work.

I had a correspondent named London Line Dave. He was a navigator on a Hercules airplane. He would go to England on a regular basis and he was a big music fan. He would bring back records that weren't released anywhere else, and we would play them as hits-to-be. He would also get me interview clips with artists because I gave him a letter on letterhead saying he was my official correspondent in the U.K.

JH: You must have MC'd some very cool shows back in those days.

AP: I was hosting the Jimi Hendrix show at the Capitol Theatre in 1968. The opening group finished, and people were waiting, I went backstage and see what was taking them so long to come out. So I go back, and the smoke in that dressing room was so thick you could cut it with scissors. They were just smoking it up. I said, "Hey guys. The fans are waiting and they're clapping." They looked up at me with half-opened eyes and said, "Uh, where are we?" But they went out, did their thing and played, and looked stone cold sober. Those were the days.

JH: *The Final Hour* was my favourite show. You'd hear long album tracks late at night that would later become the cornerstone of FM free form radio. Where did that idea come from?

AP: I figured the kids were dropping off by ten because they had school the next day, so let's play some of the album cuts and longer versions of the current hits for the older kids. I met this guy named Brian Murphy at the Treble Clef. He had a very astute knowledge of what was going on in music, a lot more than all of me combined. He said we should be playing some of these longer tracks from albums, so I gave him the spotlight to see what he could do with it. Brian was occasionally consulted for input due to his knowledge of the 'underground' music at the time. I gradually worked him in as a guest host. People liked it. It was a great chance to expose this kind of music. I remember that Kathleen Ryan, who was the wife of CFRA founder Frank Ryan, said she loved a song I played late at night. She said it was a long song and she really enjoyed it. It turned out to be "Alice's Restaurant" by

Arlo Guthrie. You can't play those cuts during the day, so we just roped off time for *The Final Hour*.

> **NEWSLETTER**
>
> **10 – 11 p.m. WEEK NIGHTS ON CFRA**
> **ALEXANDER PASCAL presents "THE FINAL HOUR"**
> Ottawa's Youth Speaks Out . . .
> "I am writing this letter while "freaking out" with your Final Hour. From 10 - 11 has become one of the best hours of the day for me."
> "I think it is a mature program that reflects the taste of our times, in a fascinating manner."
> "I must thank you once more on behalf of all of us who listen to the "final hour" with appreciation for your fantastic understanding of the Twilight Zone of 20 to 25 years old."
> "The Final Hour - a breakthrough in radio broadcasting."
> "The Final Hour is my highlight of the day."
> "I think the Final Hour is a blending of many things, and each individual will extract from it a meaning and message of their own - a diversity of convictions, in a unity of spirit, and somehow symbolic of the oneness of all youth. The Final Hour has substantiated my feelings on this oneness - I thank you."
> "The final hour is a very versatile program composed of songs not normally heard, chosen by the audience."
> **Don't miss "The Final Hour" - - 10 – 11 p.m.**
> **The "Now Sound" of CFRA - dial 580**

After *The Final Hour* was dropped by CFRA in 1969, Brian Murphy retuned to his duties at Treble Clef, but thankfully his radio career was just beginning.

Unlike other major Canadian cities, Ottawa had no cool FM rock radio station when the '70s arrived. Toronto had CHUM-FM and Montreal had the legendary CHOM-FM, but Ottawa would have to wait till 1975 when CKCU-FM Radio Carleton arrived. Then came CHEZ-FM in 1977.

The unexpected opportunity for "Murph" came in the early '70s, when he was offered a late-night shift on Ted Daigle's CKBY-FM country music station. *Free Form Radio* ran Sunday nights from 10 p.m. to midnight and was the perfect showcase for Brian. He was certainly no huge, radio megastar like Al Pascal or Gord Atkinson, but if you were *really* into cutting-edge, alternative music, Murph was "The Source."

In 1977, mentor and friend Harvey Glatt brought Brian on board for the launch of his new FM station CHEZ106 as the station's first music director. He later hosted three legendary shows on Sunday nights: *The Source*, *Blues 106* and *Jazz 106*.

THINK of somebody to-night, He'll be thinking of you!

BRIAN MURPHY
FREE FORM RADIO
DIAL 105.3 CKBY FM
SUNDAY 10 pm to 12 midnight

SIR JOHN A. RECORDS

Most of the records DJs played in the 1960s came from the major record labels of the day. But a very select few were on smaller, independent labels.

The history of indie record labels goes back to the 1930s. Stories abound about entrepreneurs driving the backroads of North America with their car trunks full of records featuring regional artists who couldn't find a home on the big-city record labels. They may have been Black, or they may have been country artists who were "too hick" for the majors, but they had solid followings in the rural towns and juke joints.

It was not an overly respectable business. These label bosses would usually handle the recording sessions as well as the pressing of the discs and the distribution. A couple of bucks in the right hands might result in some radio airplay, but it was mostly the car deliveries to record stores that made the money, which the artists rarely saw.

This practice continued throughout the '50s, when many Black artists were shunned by the majors but still gained popularity through radio stations throughout the south. Sun Records was one of the most successful and famous indie labels of the '50s, thanks to recordings by Elvis, Johnny Cash, Carl Perkins and Jerry Lee Lewis. In Chicago, Chess Records had Chuck Berry, Howlin' Wolf, Muddy Waters and other blues and R&B greats.

In Ottawa, we had Diana Records run by Ralph Mongeau. It started as a country label but went rock when they released a single by The Darnells, who would evolve into The Townsmen. The Darnells also backed up the team of Laurie and Diane for two more releases on Diana. The Skaliwags chose Excellent Records as their recording home.

The boldest and most successful label was Sir John A., created by CJET DJ John Pozer and Ron Greene from Don Norman and the Other

Four, in large part because of bad experiences with major label support of Ottawa groups.

Pozer was an incredible ball of energy and creativity. He was well known to Ottawa music fans for his radio gig and for his stint as host of the teen dance show *Saturday Date*, loosely patterned after Dick Clark's *American Bandstand*. Pozer was also the managerial force behind the 5D, The Eyes of Dawn and Don Norman and the Other Four. No surprise those three bands were the cornerstones of Sir John A.'s recording roster.

To their credit, John and Ron realized the limitations and challenges of their endeavour. While the temptation might have been there to sign up a slew of artists and flood the market with product while record buyers were ready and willing to shell out cash for singles, they decided to take a more measured and tactical course. The idea was to be very selective with their products and to aim high with every release. Pressings were limited to save money, and between 1966 – 1969 Sir John A. only released a grand total of fourteen records from eight artists: The 5D, Don Norman and the Other Four, Thee Deuces (later known as The Hearts), The Eastern Passage, The Eyes of Dawn, Those Naughty Boys, Jay Telfer and The Paper Dream.

The process, from choice of material through to stocking the stores, ran like clockwork. Pozer, Greene and usually Don Norman would help pick the material for the releases. Then it was off to Montreal to record, mixing usually happened in Toronto, and then the records would be pressed at the RCA Victor plant in Smiths Falls. They would then be packaged, usually with picture sleeves, and then Don would throw the boxes in his car and drop them off at Treble Clef, Sherman's Musicland and other local and Valley stores.

With Pozer's pull and the general quality of the recordings, radio play in Ottawa was virtually assured, and a distribution deal with RCA saw the discs shipped out across the country, resulting in some great chart success outside Ottawa. The Eyes of Dawn's version of Dusty Springfield's hit "Little By Little," sung by fifteen-year-old bassist Rick Lemieux, even picked up radio play in Detroit. The 5D, with "Baby Boy" and "Running Round in Circles," and Don Norman and the Other Four, with "Low Man," both had #1 songs on *The Swing Set*, and pretty well all the Sir John A. releases cracked the Top 30.

It was a remarkable track record for an indie label, but unfortunately the label's run was short. Pozer landed a job in the record business in Toronto, where he had moved to help push the 5D to greater heights. Then the 5D broke up and Sir John A. was left without their major act. In 1968, The Paper Dream released the last single on the label, and Sir John A. faded into the shadows of history.

SOME "IDOL CHATTER" WITH HY BLOOM

There were basically three options for making records in the early '60s. Toronto had the best facilities, but that was an expensive trip and reserved for the bands like The Esquires.

The second option was Montreal. That option was closer and cheaper, and several of Ottawa's top bands made that trip.

And for the bands who just wanted something clean and simple to peddle as a demo, for a rather pricey $12 an hour, there was Hy Bloom.

Walking into Hy Bloom's recording studio at 283 Bank Street was like entering a time tunnel. No comfy chairs or ferns in this office, just wall-to-wall, ceiling-to-floor stacks of amplifiers, speakers, tapes, electrical parts and things that go "beep." And sitting on a chair in the midst of this electronic cacophony sat the man himself...Hy Bloom.

Harry Hyman (Hy) Bloom was an Ottawa boy who learned the recording craft by being a "studio rat" in the finest recording studios in New York City. Thankfully he came home to share his gift, forming a company he called Soundmaster.

Although he did most of his work with country, classical and jazz artists in his early days, when rock and roll hit, he was flooded with requests for sessions because he was basically the only guy in town with a real recording studio. This is long, long before DIY records.

A lot of great records came out of Hy Bloom's studio, no matter how much he disliked working with rock and roll bands.

> **JH:** You started out recording jazz and classical groups. Tell us about your rock and roll experience.
>
> **HB:** I wasn't happy with rock and roll. I found out the best way to record most groups was to place them in a circle so that that faced each other. This was especially important in jazz where it's key to look at each other to get your cues. It's the best way for a group to play together. First of all, I couldn't get the rock bands to look at each other. They would all line up like soldiers in a row. I would listen to the tape playback and hear that the drummer and bass player weren't playing together. I'd play it back for them and a riot would start in the studio. The drummer would say "I'm the drummer. Everybody follows me." I actually had bands that broke up in the studio because they couldn't work together. I could put an echo effect on them to make them sound better, but they were always out of tune. They were crap. They were garbage! It became one disaster after another. I did a lot of those groups. Record labels would call me and ask me to send them the demos that had some promise. Some did, but these bands could never get a second good one, and that's what the record companies wanted because they were in it to make money.
>
> **JH:** George Martin was not a big fan of rock and roll either, but he worked with The Beatles and was instrumental in making them the biggest band in the world. Despite your feelings about the music, did you ever think about taking a local band under your wing and moulding them into stars?

HB: For me The Beatles were real musicians. They could read music, they were trained. But kids their age thought all they had to do was buy a guitar, learn some chords and become a musician. I never found a group yet that could do it. My idea of recording is that if you didn't get it on the first or second take, you give up and go to the next song and come back to it later or the next day. Music has to be fresh from the soul. It got to the point when we had sixteen tracks that musicians would listen back and say they wanted to do their part again because one note was a bit off. They don't care about the overall band song of the recording, just their own part. I kept that sixteen-track recorder for about six months then I gave it away. I got sick and tired of those god-damned rock musicians coming back to do all these takes again. I worked with country bands here in Ottawa that would come in prepared and produce a full album in ninety minutes. It got to the point where I would work with some bands for an hour then tell then to go home and practice and come back when they are ready to do a real professional demo. In the early '80s I just gave up on the rock and roll thing.

JH: Did Paul Anka ever record with you in his early days?

HB: No. But he worked at his dad's café on Bank and he used to bring us coffee. He was a nice kid, I liked him, but we never recorded together. He had a cousin here in Ottawa called Bobby Anka. His dad owned a restaurant on Bank called Stagedoor. Now Bobby could sing a little, so his dad paid me big money to record Bobby and see what came out of it. So I brought in some pro musicians to back him up and do a session. It didn't go well. What Bobby turned out sounded like crap. So after the session I kept Bobby and his dad behind while the musicians packed up. I said to him, "Bobby. What are you trying to achieve here?" And Bobby said, "I know I can't sing as well as Paul, and I'm never going to be a big star like Paul. But if I can be 25% as good and make 25% as much money as Paul, I will be happy."

JH: I heard that some sessions were interrupted by the streetcars going by on Bank.

HB: I got that problem beat after a while. I had a microphone in the window and when I heard the streetcar bell down the road, I would stop the session and give the boys a break. The funniest part was watching these young kids hauling their Hammond organs and drums up the long flight of stairs to get to the studio. They never complained, though.

JH: You did some early work with The Staccatos.

HB: Well, Dean Hagopian was a very funny guy with a really great following on the radio. One day he wanted to sing this song, he had a pretty good voice, with The Staccatos. So, they booked time in the studio. Turns out the song was very serious. They practised it, and when we went to record, Dean took off his shoes. Then he took of his trousers. He had trouble with the shorts, but the song was a disaster and they didn't try again. Dean just couldn't control himself. You got to love him. And I think I have the tape here somewhere. I think it's the only time we had a striptease in the studio.

Hy Bloom passed away shortly after I talked to him in 2017. He told me he was worried about what would happen to his irreplaceable tape collection when he passed on. The tapes are now safe and secure in the Ottawa Archives. He would be very, very happy about that.

THE 5D

Despite the fact that he played bass in one of the more successful bands of the mid- to late '60s, Brad Campbell describes the 5D as "a middling pop band." But thanks to some good breaks, a solid work ethic and a hell of a manager, the 5D produced some of the best records of the time and came closer than most to breaking through on the Toronto scene.

Dave Poulin and Brad Campbell were children of The Beatles. They talked on the phone the night of that Sullivan show, and pretty well decided there and then to start up a band. Like most aspiring rock stars, they first started jamming with their friends, but, as Brad recalls, that process didn't work out well. "The other guys didn't really work at it, or stick with us. From then on it was a process of getting better people in the band. It was always Dave and I getting people around us."

Slowly, the Fifth Dimension, as they were then called, began to get gigs, but still the process of finding the right chemistry continued. "We were just another band that was hacking away doing the top 40 or whatever was on that chart. It's what everybody did," says Dave. "I'm not sure what separated us from the other bands. It might have been our professionalism. Dave always wanted us to be a pro band."

After many experiments with personnel, they found guitarist Keith Richardson, who had been with the wonderfully named Terry Webb and the Spiders. It was that core of three who would power the Fifth Dimension for the years to come. But first there was a major bump in the road they had to navigate.

It was all over the radio in 1966. "Up, up and away-eee-ay, in my beautiful, my beautiful balloooooooon!" "Up, Up and Away" was one of the biggest hits of '66. It was one of many for the California-based Fifth Dimension. There was no question that somewhere down the road, this would be problematic. The Ottawa Fifth Dimension needed a new name. They felt it shouldn't be too far away from the old name since they had developed a solid following around town, so they chose the shorter 5D.

With their spot-on cover songs, the gigs came easily that year. "First you'd be going to Buckingham, Thurso and Masson. Then the next weekend Pembroke, Renfrew, Arnprior, Cobden and so on," Brad remembers. "You'd have a couple of gigs a weekend going through the booking agencies. We were young guys getting up to $500 a night." There were so many bands from both Ottawa and Gatineau that club owners were fighting each other to get the best ones. And that competition meant more money for the groups.

But Dave, Brad and Keith had a hankering to take the next step and do some recording. The only problem was they had no good original material. It looked like the 5D's balloon was deflating. But in stepped John Pozer.

Pozer was still a crackerjack manager, but now he had a new baby… Sir John A. Records. He was looking for good bands, and lack of original material was not a major stumbling block. Look what The Townsmen had done in that same situation. John and the boys started scrounging through the record bins for cool tunes that were unknown to the listening audience. They struck paydirt with the first single.

Bye, bye, "Fifth Dimension"

Brad says he still loves "Baby Boy." "I remember the first time it was played on the radio. We were driving along in this piece-of-junk car with the one speaker in the dashboard. It was such a thrill. It was the perfect summer, blast-out-of-the-radio kind of tune. I don't even know whose song it was originally. It sounded very British, as did most other stuff at the time. I'm surprised we weren't singing in British accents on that one. Everybody wanted to be British. 'Running Round in Circles' was the same thing. It was originally done by a British band called The Ivy League. John had heard their version and he gave it to us and basically said, 'Here. Do this one.' It was a big hit in Ottawa."

The 5D was one of the best-sounding studio bands in the city, and with a little luck and airplay in the right places, they could have broken out nationally. Right off the bat, The 5D and Don Norman and the Other Four stood atop the pecking order at Sir John A. Records.

Pozer showed incredible confidence in the band when he unveiled the next step for the group. He was taking them to Toronto to make the big time! Brad tells the story.

"If it wasn't for John Pozer, we wouldn't be talking today. The band was good, but John Pozer was extraordinary. If you look at the gigs he got this rather middling pop band, it's amazing. We opened for Wilson Pickett at Massey Hall in Toronto, and at the Capitol Theatre in Ottawa along with Bruce Cockburn's new band The Flying Circus. We had no business doing that Massey Hall show. We're up there doing pop music we didn't even write. John had us doing TV shows. We played for the Queen in 1967. Our last gig was opening for The Who at the Civic Centre, the first show there. This was all because John Pozer was our manager. He would just go out there and kick open doors. We would walk in and do what we did. We all moved to Toronto and lived in a house and tried to make our marks."

Sadly, that didn't happen. Pozer found a new job in the music business in Toronto and the 5D returned home to Ottawa. After that 1968 opening gig for The Who, they packed it in. In a move of pure chutzpah, the 5D hired a small orchestra for their rendition of the Richard Harris epic "MacArthur Park." They went out with a bang!

Poulin, Campbell and Richardson played several reunion shows and never lost touch. They formed a new called The Yohawks in the 2010s. With Richardson no longer with us, Brad and Dave continue to make music, just like they promised to do that Sunday night in 1964.

JULY 16, 1968:
THE WHO ROCK THE CIVIC CENTRE

The Ottawa Civic Centre at Lansdowne Park was built primarily to house the Ottawa 67's hockey team, but it also became the go-to venue for rock concerts for the next thirty years. The first rock show was held on July16, 1968, and was billed as "Ottawa's Greatest Show Ever."

Opening the evening of madness and merriment was Ottawa's 5D, followed by American bubblegummers The Ohio Express, British garage-rockers The Troggs and then, headlining, The Who. Tickets were $2.50.

In those days, it was impossible to follow The Who. This was at the height of their instrument-smashing phase. When The Who was done, all that was left was smoke and smashed equipment.

Doug McKeen was handling sound for that show and remembers the night well.

> **DOUG MCKEEN (SOUND ENGINEER):** *This was during the time that they wrecked equipment. They smashed their guitars, the drum set, and pretty well all the sound equipment.*
>
> *Now we were doing the sound system for the show. This was a big gig, the first rock show at the Civic Centre. We had*

bought all new microphones, all new microphone stands. We had paid pretty big money for this stuff.

When the band arrived, we talked to the road manager and said, we know you wreck all your stuff, but what happens to our equipment? He said, 'No, no. We leave your stuff alone. We have special guitars for the second part of the show. They fall apart really easily. We wreck them every night.'

So, I talked with my partner and said there's no way they're not going to wreck our stuff. So, we came up with plan B.

At the end of the night, sure enough, our microphone stands weren't straight up and down, they bent them all around. They had thrown all the microphones into the audience, they were gone. The guy had bullshitted us. We put plan B into operation.

As soon as the band left the stage, we took all of their amplifiers and threw them under the stage. We knew The Who was playing the next night in Montreal, so they had to leave pretty quickly. Off they went without their amps.

Next day we got a phone call from the road manager asking if we'd noticed any amplifiers lying around. And we said 'The Who? Never heard of ya.' Then we sold off the amps and bought new microphones and stands.

But the story doesn't end there.

Years later, Doug and his wife were on vacation in England. They went out to a fancy London restaurant, and who should be there but Pete Townshend! Doug worked up the courage to drop over and recounted the "lost amp" story. Doug owned up to being the culprit and waited for the repercussions. Pete just laughed and replied, "We travelled the world many times and you're the only guy that figured it out and got even with us."

THE EYES OF DAWN

It was hard to miss The Eyes of Dawn driving around town. They had an equipment van, of course, but theirs was different. It had a huge eye on the side, like something off the streets of psychedelic London.

The band was one of the later signings for Sir John A. Records, and there were great hopes from both parties that they would be the next 5D as far as success went.

They first caught the ear of John Pozer during a long house stint at a café in Hull called La Petite Souris, which was always packed for their performances. Then the Sir John A. machine took over, and The Eyes of Dawn were whisked off to RCA Studios in Montreal where they recorded their first single, "Time to Be Going," under the watchful eye and ears of Don Norman and Ron Greene. Like the early 5D material, "Time to Be Going" was a cover of an obscure British single by The Fortunes.

Just after its release, the band had a personnel shuffle, which was due more to over-indulgence than creative differences. Bassist Rick Lemieux was the guy who is the right place at the right time.

Rick has started off playing the guitar his mom bought for him. But then he says he "got bitten by the bass bug because it was so much easier to play. I bought an old bass and started jamming with friends. We would take the bus to hang out at Parkdale United Church and St. Elizabeth Church to hear bands."

One of the bands he loved was The Eyes of Dawn, and he became friends with the guys and was soon a familiar face at gigs and even practices. Maybe in the far back of his mind was the thought that maybe someday he could work his way into the group and play alongside his idol, singer Terry King. The chance for that to happen came in a most unexpected manner.

The Eyes of Dawn ready for action

"'Time to be Going' did really well in the Ottawa area before I arrived," he remembers. "Then one night while the band was practising, there was some drinking going on and they got into a fight." When the dust settled, lead singer Wayne McQuaid had quit. "So here they were. The record was still on the charts without a lead singer. They asked me if I knew any of their songs and I said, 'Actually, I know all your songs,' because I hung around the band a lot. So, Terry King moved from bass to lead singer and I took over on bass. I was fifteen years old. I lied about my age because at that age I could not have gotten into the Musicians Union. Then we brought in Jack Arsenault, who had been with the 5D on keyboards and guitar."

Terry took an instant liking to the kid and became a huge influence. "If there was one person who was very influential for me, it was Terry King. He had a very brusque personality, but he was super, super nice and a great singer and musician. He taught me about harmonies, and I think I learned most of my chords through him. Terry went on to play with Les Emmerson and The Cooper Brothers."

After another personnel shuffle, Pozer shuffled the band off to Montreal again to record the second single. Again, it was a British cover, but this time, nearly-sixteen-year-old Rick Lemieux was handling the vocals. The song was Dusty Springfield's "Little by Little," and it is one of the best songs to come out on Sir John A. It even got picked up by a radio station in Detroit.

Opening for the Animals at that memorable Coliseum gig in 1967 was interesting, as was the opening slot for Roy Orbison that year at the Capitol Theatre. But despite the hopes and dreams of John Pozer, The Eyes of Dawn broke up early in 1969 with members scattered to the wind and new careers.

The Eyes of Dawn never got beyond the role of a solid live act, but that kept them busy enough in a live music market that rarely slept.

ONE NIGHT IN THE CAPITAL

In the 1960s there was no reason not to go out and have some fun on a Friday or Saturday night. The entertainment menu ran from floor shows, to showbands, to "international singing sensations," to folk clubs, to rock and roll.

On the night of June 17, 1966, you could catch the legendary Valley band The Happy Wanderers at the Alexandra Hotel; Bobby Brown and the Curios at the Riverside Hotel; Fawzira Amir, "direct from the Sahara," at the Greber Hotel; Roland Legault and the Trio at the Chez Henri Hotel; Jack McPartlin at the Duvernay Motor Hotel; or Dolly Lyons and the Fabulous Talisman Go-Go Girls at the Talisman Hotel.

"And for the youngsters…" as Ed Sullivan was fond of saying, these local rock bands were all in action that one night.

THE STACCATOS…Walkley Road Arena

THE CHILDREN…Pineland

THE FIFTH DIMENSION (5D)…Smiths Falls Community Centre

THE RAPHAELS…Almonte Town Hall

THE SKALIWAGS…The Groove, Strand Hall

DON NORMAN AND THE OTHER FOUR…Woodroffe High School

THEE DEUCES…Nepean High School

THOSE NAUGHTY BOYS…United Church Hall, Arnprior

THE CHARACTERS…Knight of Columbus, Eastview

THE BARONS…St. Richard's Church Hall

THEE GROUP…The Roost, Eastview Recreation Centre

THE TOWNSMEN…Talisman Motor Hotel

UNIT FIVE…Our Lady of Mount Carmel

And if you had any energy left, and $1.25, the next night there was a "raucous 12-band thrash" at the Ottawa Coliseum to celebrate the end of exams. On the bill were The Esquires, The Skaliwags, The Barons, The Children, The Trippers, Thee Deuces, The Townsmen, The Scoundrels, The Raphaels, Eyes of Dawn, Thee Group and Don Norman and the Other Four. The concert ran twelve straight hours from noon to midnight.

Here are some of the other hot spots to play in the area in the '60s. This is list is courtesy of local music historian, musician, and uber-fan Ken Creighton.

Attic (The) – 248 Bank St. between Lisgar & Cooper

The Attic
dancing nightly!
Home of
The Morning Glory
248 BANK ST.
BETWEEN LISGAR & COOPER
CLOSED SUNDAY – OPEN MONDAY TO FRIDAY

MORNING GLORY TO APPEAR ON SATURDAY
DATE ON JULY 15

Barn (The) – Aylmer

Bistro 1060 – 1060 Wellington Street

Brown Jug (The) – 1915 Bank Street – near Alta Vista

Canterbury Community Centre – Arch Street

```
CANTERBURY COMMUNITY CENTRE
         ARCH STREET
          PRESENTS
       THE FABULOUS
      STYTCH IN TIME
         FROM TORONTO

     SATURDAY, APRIL 13th
   NO 61 BUS TAKES YOU TO THE DOOR

   BOOKED BY  East West
                    163 METCALFE ST.,
                    SUITE 302,
                    OTTAWA 4, ONTARIO
                    PHONE (613) 236-8830
```

Chaudière "Snake Pit"

Establishment (The) – Lakeside Gardens, Britannia Park: *"Dress will be jackets & ties but bring your swimsuit for an afternoon swim in Britannia Bay. Spend the whole day at the beach and the evening at The Establishment. A nice place to take your favourite girl, or meet a new one."* (Ottawa *Swing Set*, June 30, 1967)

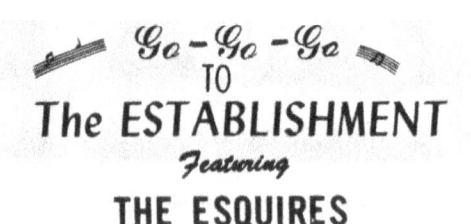

> **Go-Go-Go TO**
> # The ESTABLISHMENT
> *Featuring*
> ## THE ESQUIRES
> MARCH 26th, $1.00 Per Person

Funk and Soul – 412 Preston Street

Glebe Collegiate Auditorium

Glenwood Bowl – Glenwood Shopping Centre Aylmer, P.Q. (The Place)

> SUNDAY, AUGUST 28   –   9 – 12 p.m.
> **GLENWOOD BOWL**
> PRESENTS
> OTTAWA'S FAVOURITE
> ## THE SCOUNDRELS
> Dress: Casual but Neat $1.00 per Person

Groove (The) – Strand Hall, Bank Street

Gyrostat (The) – 135 Eddy Street, Hull: *"The Gyrostat has everything. Three floors of entertainment. The first floor contains the only Roller Skating Rink in Ottawa or Hull, the second floor has eight bowling lanes and a large sit down restaurant. Every Saturday and Sunday, top bands appear on the third floor."* (Ottawa *Swing Set*, December 8, 1967)

> **THE GYROSTAT**
> (WHERE IT'S AT)
> THE ACTION THIS WEEK
>
> SUNDAY, AUG. 27 – THE HEART
> SIR JOHN A
> RECORDING ARTIST
> THE RAPHAELS
> 6 VOICES
>
> M.C. CFRA's PAUL LOUGHEED
> 8:30 – 11:30 $1.25
>
> WHERE THE ACTION IS NEXT WEEK
> ON SEPT. 4 8–11   THE TOWNSMEN
> THE OUTCAST

Hub (The) – Centennial Centre, 2 Rideau Street

Knights of Columbus – Eastview

Lantern

Le Hibou – 521 Sussex Dr.

> *Sunday A-Go-Go*
> at LE HIBOU
> 521 Sussex Dr.
> EVERY SUNDAY From 2 - 5 p.m.
>
> *Featuring Ottawas' Top Groups*
> The TOWNSMEN
> The ESQUIRES
> The CHILDREN
> The SCOUNDRELS
>
> $1.00 per person   Membership Available
> REGULAR LE HIBOU MEMBERSHIP HONORED

Oak Door (The) – 485 Bank Street

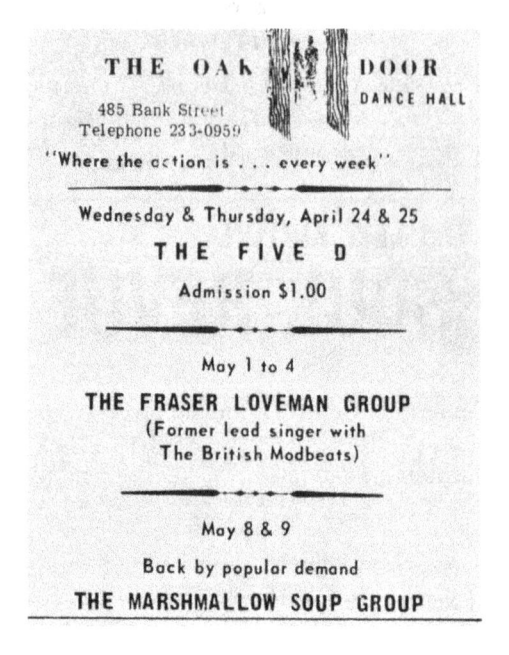

> **THE OAK DOOR DANCE HALL**
> 485 Bank Street
> Telephone 233-0959
> "Where the action is . . . every week"
>
> Wednesday & Thursday, April 24 & 25
> **THE FIVE D**
> Admission $1.00
>
> May 1 to 4
> **THE FRASER LOVEMAN GROUP**
> (Former lead singer with
> The British Modbeats)
>
> May 8 & 9
> Back by popular demand
> **THE MARSHMALLOW SOUP GROUP**

The Ottawa House

Parkdale United Church

Pinegroove Pineland, across from the Hunt Club

Pink Panther Club – King Edward at Murray

> **Teen 'n Twenty Club**
> **THE PINK PANTHER**
> Opening April 8
> 256 King Edward Ave

Roost (The) – Eastview Recreation Centre

RYC – 1940 Saunderson Drive

St. Augustine's Church – Baseline at Merivale

St. George's Church Hall – Metcalfe and Gloucester with the Saturday night "Record Hop"

St. Martin's Church – (behind Carlingwood Shopping Centre)

Strand Hall – Bank & Riverdale

Tower (The) – 2345 Alta Vista Drive (St. Thomas The Apostle Church)

> **THE TOWER** (Ottawa's No. 1 Dance)
> **ST. THOMAS APOSTLE CHURCH**
> corner of **ALTA VISTA**
> and **RANDALL**
>
> **FRIDAY**
> **MAY 5**
> thee exciting
> "HEART"
> Formerly "THEE DEUCES"
>
> AND PAUL LOUGHEED
> of YOUNG TEMPO TIME
> & THE CAMPUS CLUB
>
> COME EARLY!
> (Last 2 dances were sellouts)
> $1.00 per person
> casual but neat
> 8:30-12 midnight

Uplands Airmen's Club

Walkley Road Arena

THE EASTERN PASSAGE

So near, and yet so far. That is the bottom line for the saga of The Eastern Passage. While they managed to create a solid following in Ottawa, a contract with Sir John A. Records, management with Don Billows and even some radio airplay in the States, The Eastern Passage was destined to stay north of the 49th.

The roots of the group lie in the hallways of Rideau High School in the early '60s, where John Lacasse started up his first band, The Telstars, named for the hit instrumental by the British band The Tornados. Again, this was the era when instrumental bands were the coolest thing.

The Telstars get to stay up late on a weeknight

Like DJ Dean Hagopian with his Staccatos, John Pozer decided to take advantage of his fame and try life on the performance side with his own backup group. He chose the Telstars. When that project failed to produce any gold records, the Telstars became The In-Crowd, named, again, after a popular current song. One more change gave us the familiar "Eastern Passage."

With former Hi-Tone Don Billows handling the management, The Eastern Passage played regular gigs at his club the Oak Door, and soon caught the attention of their old lead singer John Pozer. Pozer signed the band to Sir John A. It proved to be a brief relationship.

Like most other Sir John A. bands, a cover tune was chosen for their first single. The song was "When You Ask About Love," a lesser known tune by The Crickets. It did not set the radio waves, or the music world, on fire.

Rather than let the disappointment faze them, the group and Billows doubled down on the second single. Instead of relying on others to make them stars, they took a unique, DIY approach, which was highly unusual for the time. The started their own label, Zoo Records in 1968, recorded "I Feel So Fine," and started shopping the record around to major record labels. Warner Brothers agreed to an international distribution deal, several American stations started to play the record, and the champagne corks popped!

But, as has happened so often, the record company moved on to new sounds as the music world forged ahead at breakneck speed, and The Eastern Passage project was put on the back burner. They had come as close to becoming Ottawa's first breakthrough band as anyone before, but, as Maxwell Smart would say, "Missed by that much!"

It had to be deflating to go back to square one, but that's what The Eastern Passage did for the next two years, playing the same clubs and dances they had before America came calling. Still, they gave the dream a real solid shot, and for that we say, good on them!

SCOUNDRELZ AND SKALIWAGS, OH MY!

In the early '60s, there was no shortage of what Brad Campbell of the 5D calls "jukebox bands." That would change around 1967 when most groups realized they had to write at least some of their own material if they wanted any chance to make the big time. Before then, it was all about song-recognition. That was the difference between a packed house and a quiet night.

The Scoundrelz, before the "Z"

The Scoundrelz managed to attract crowds, not only with their repertoire of the big hits of the day, but also with a stage show that defied description, especially for their times.

The band began life as The Tartans. Guess what kind of outfits they wore? Marc Corbin and his brother were founding members, but before long Marc fired his brother and brought in drummer Kenny Chapman and some other friends from Woodroffe High School. The lineup that began gigging featured Marc, Kenny, Buddy Stanton on rhythm guitar, Mike Provost on vocals and sax player Bob Duffy. No bass player.

"The very first place we played was St. Basil's Church and we got five bucks apiece. We all wore the tartan outfits," Buddy remembers. "We were doing pretty well all instrumental stuff, but you could see that was coming to an end real quick. The music coming out after The Beatles had nothing to do with saxophone music, so we had to let Bob go."

In came bass player Rick Lemieux, who would later join The Eastern Passage. It was time to update the set list, and not surprisingly, tunes by The Beatles and the Stones were highlights. Buddy was a die-hard Fab Four fan. "Like most kids in Ottawa, I got into rock and roll when The Beatles arrived on the scene. I remember getting that first album and I couldn't believe all the chords. I just sat in the basement and learned all the tunes and thought that these guys were really good. This was a long way from Bill Haley."

The Tartans were making a bit of money by now and were good enough to attract the attention of both Sandy Gardner and leading booking agent Lennie Alexander. The next tick in the box was getting a new moniker. According to Buddy, "Mike Provost called me one day and asked what I thought about the name The Tartans. I said, 'Not much.' He said there was a famous racehorse he had read about in the States called The Scoundrel, and Mike thought it was a great band name. So, we became The Scoundrels with an 'S.' But when we were talking about making our first record, we were told there was a group in upstate New York called The Scoundrels, and they had the name first. We talked about a wholesale name change, but Sandy Gardiner convinced us that it would be better to forget that idea because the name had some recognition now in the Ottawa market. Well,

The Beatles had altered the spelling of 'Beetles' and The Byrds were hot, so we just added the 'Z' and became The Scoundrelz. Problem solved."

Sandy, as usual, was right. The new Scoundrelz band rolled on as if nothing had happened. The fanbase stayed with them and grew by the gig. Buddy remembers a show at St. Augustine's Church. "The hall was good for 300 people, but when they got over 1,000 people in there somebody from the church called the fire department to clear the place out. We played a Battle of the Bands at the Auditorium, and they should have brought the fire department in for that one too. It was all local bands. It was twelve hours of music and it was jammed. There was enough talent working in those days in Ottawa to put on something like that. Everybody went to dances on the weekend. Everybody! Live rock and roll bands in Ottawa were rivalling bingo for the churches. They were making a good buck off us. We did have a really good following, and there was no social media. It was just word of mouth." And that "word of mouth" was about to get even louder.

It was their manager who found the right song for that all-important first single on the Toronto-based Red Leaf Label. "Sandy came to me and said we gotta make a record. We were making lots of cash in church basements, but it was time to go into the studio," says Buddy. "He suggested we do 'Heartbreak Hotel' by Elvis. I took the song and turned it around and it worked. The flip side was a song I wrote called 'Poor John,' which was written around the strength of our vocals. We were really at the top of our game at that point with our harmonies. The two songs were in the race for Gord Atkinson's "hit parade" for #1 and #2. Those were heady times for a bunch of kids!"

Marc Corbin says of "Heartbreak Hotel," "I'm proud of that song. I think it still holds its place in time and could be played now." It certainly ranks in my top five local tunes of that period.

"Heartbreak Hotel" and "Poor John" blasted out of radios all over town in the fall of 1965. Sandy Gardiner plugged their every gig in his column, and the crowds got bigger and bigger. Mike Provost had developed into one of the best, if not the best, frontman in town, with a flair for the dramatic and that natural ability to control an audience. And then there were the outfits.

At first, The Scoundrelz dressed like The Beach Boys and did fairly standard stage choreography. But one night at the Britannia Yacht Club, it all changed. Buddy remembers it well. "The show was going over okay during the first set, but it was more an Elvis place than a Beatles place. We went back to the dressing room, and I guess they had plays there because there were a whole bunch of costumes. Now Provost had a theatrical streak in him a mile wide, so he starts going through the stuff and talks us into dressing up for the second set. Mike introduced us as The Sparkle Rockets, and we all had on these ridiculous outfits. Some people caught on to the gag, but quite a few people thought these guys were way better than the first band. We were playing Elvis stuff, and it started as a goofy kind of joke, but it went down really well."

But it didn't stop with the costumes, as guitarist Mark Corbin says. "It wasn't anything that was planned. It just kind of happened. I was into the Bowery Boys and Walt Disney's *Treasure Island*, so we created our own kind of language on stage. We made our own strobe light out of a record player. We had this board on the record player with some holes in it and a light behind it. We'd stop a song in the middle and the roadie would come out and do a butt dance, shaking his butt, while we turned on the light show. It was insanity in a way and off-the-cuff."

Instead of following the lead of other bands and shopping for the latest rock fashions at Chuck Delfino's men's wear, The Scoundrelz had their outfits made for them in the shop. Once again, Mark Corbin: "We played Lansdowne Park in the Coliseum opening for the Barbarians and The Staccatos. We had on these pants that were multi-coloured, and they could have been used as drapes in somebody's horrible living room. We were taking it to the limit all the time and trying to outdo the other bands and each other. It was just having fun."

Brad Campbell of the 5D was a Scoundrelz fan. "These guys would go out on Friday night and wear outfits made from drapery fabric. They looked like bright flashes of colour, and their stage antics were great. It was a whole new kind of 'show' coming from these guys."

But, as always, the show has got to end. According to Buddy Stanton, "As much as anything, I think it was my fault. Sandy came to us and told us we had to record again. I think by that time we were on a gentle glide-path downwards, and I just thought, I don't want to do this. At the same time, I was getting phone calls from The Townsmen. They had just revamped their band and they had brought in Johnny Bacho from The Skaliwags. We had been friends for a long time, and he and Frank Morrison kept calling saying The Scoundrelz weren't that good anymore and that I should come over to The Townsmen. I told the guys after we got back from Montreal where we recorded the next single. They didn't replace me. Everyone just kind of drifted off to other bands. Marc went to the 5D and Rick went to The Eastern Passage. It seemed our time was up."

The Skaliwags

The breakup was also disappointing for Mark Corbin. "When Buddy left, the band just lost its fuse. John Pozer approached me and asked me to join the 5D. I said sure, somebody wants me to play, let's go. Deep down we loved each other and loved what we did."

Johnny Bacho also loved what he did with his band The Skaliwags. "It was a fantastic time. I wouldn't trade it for anything," he says. "The Skaliwags were great, as were all the bands I played with. The groups would all hung around together a lot. We would hang with The Scoundrelz a lot."

The Scoundrelz and Skaliwags had lots in common. They shared a love for the Stones, and for the grittier rock sound that more polished bands like The Staccatos, The Townsmen and The Esquires only dabbled in.

As The Scoundrelz began life as The Tartans, The Skaliwags, who were based in Gatineau, were first known as The Trutones, a very square name, even for 1961. In an attempt to appeal to the English crowd in Ottawa, some members adopted Anglo stage names. Andre Cote took the name Andy Cody and Gerry Fortier became Gerry Foster.

John Bacho doesn't think the band had any playing gigs under that name, but when they switched to the hipper name The Skaliwags, things started to change. "That's when we started to get bookings. We played a lot of stag parties and high schools, and then moved up to Pineland, the Battle of the Bands shows and the clubs."

The Skaliwags could have been just another "jukebox band" if they hadn't had two trump cards. Singer Ed Mitchell had his Jagger moves down pat, making the Stones material jump off the stage. And John Bacho was the kind of wicked guitar player that other musicians came out to see.

It was "Walk Don't Run" by The Ventures that inspired John to be a guitar player. "When I heard 'Walk Don't Run,' I bought the album and I bought every Ventures album after that, and I learned every song on them," he recalls. Being a leftie, it was a challenge to find a guitar he could play comfortably, till he got a custom-made Fender Stratocaster from Coulthart Music. John Bacho was 18, and ready to rock.

The '60s was the decade of guitar heroes. The Ventures, Duane Eddy, The Shadows and Dick Dale were replaced by Jimmy Page and Jeff Beck from The Yardbirds, Eric Clapton from John Mayall's Bluesbreakers, The Yardbirds and Cream, the flamboyant Pete Townshend of The Who, Keith Richards from the Stones, and, on a level of his own, another left-hander, Jimi Hendrix.

For teenage kids on the Ottawa music scene, it was time to fish or cut bait. Learning to play the right chords was only step one in the process of learning the guitar. Now you had to impress people with your originality and style. It was part of the new sound of live rock, and nobody did it better than John Bacho.

Remembered as a leading group in the "garage band" genre, The Skaliwags relied more on energy and power than tight harmonies. You can hear echoes of Paul Revere and The Raiders, and a sizzling guitar solo from John Bacho, on the first Skaliwags single in 1966, "Turn Him Down," written by their manager Paul Wharman. It was released on Excellent Records, owned by Alex Sherman of Sherman's Musicland fame, and was a #1 hit in Ottawa that winter.

Sadly, it was the only recording session with Bacho. After five years with The Skaliwags/Trutones he split for the greener pastures of The Townsmen. "I moved to The Townsmen because they were more of a vocal band," he says. "The Skaliwags were based more on the lead singer and we weren't big on harmonies. I just wanted to try something different."

The band soldiered on without John. There was one more single, "Me Minus More," but after that The Skaliwags broke up moved on to new lives. After The Townsmen, John Bacho found happiness with A Group called Bubs, who were a true bubblegum band. They would give fans sticks of gum during their shows and put on the wildest stage shows in town.

A Group Called Bubs

Like many other musicians, John Bacho's favourite place to play with The Skaliwags was on the other side of the river, just over the Chaudière Bridge. Musicians called it "The Snake Pit."

Just another night in the "Snake Pit"

GERRY BARBER: THE MAN, THE MYTH THE LEGEND

JOHN BACHO (THE SKALIWAGS:) *"Our favourite spot to play had to be downstairs at the Chaudière. Gerry Barber would always warn us if there was a fight brewing so we could hide behind our amps."*

They are the stuff of legends: Paul Bunyan, Big Joe Mufferaw, Pecos Bill. Men of extraordinary strength and daring. Men to be respected, but men to be feared. Gerry Barber was legend. The only difference is that he was real.

Was Gerry Barber the toughest guy in town? Some might say the title would go to Frank Cosenzo, the bouncer at the Riverside. If you go back a bit further you might say the dreaded Post brothers who kept order at the Oak Door. But when you talk about the guys you didn't want to mess with, Gerry Barber would likely top the list.

If you found yourself standing next to Gerry Barber, alias "Big Moose," in a club you could either breathe a sigh of relief or head for exits as fast as you could possibly move. Gerry's job was to protect the innocent and punish the guilty, and, above all, make sure his clubs were in control. Gerry was a bouncer, and he took his work very seriously.

He was born into abject poverty in the worst section of Lowertown Ottawa. His dad sold newspapers on the street corner, while his mom did her best to bring up seven kids. To bring in extra money, Gerry started bouncing at a café on Rideau Street, then he went off to do the same at a joint on Rideau Street. Working from 9 p.m. till 6 a.m., he made about $20, which wasn't bad money for those days. He made even more when he worked the wrestling shows on the Quebec side, although it was a lot more dangerous when passions got out of hand.

When he got into his early twenties, he was mixing bouncing and being a waiter at various area hotels. He finally ended up at the Chaudière Club in Gatineau, where he held court for the next thirty years. It was there Gerry Barber became a legend.

If you hung out at the Chaud, chances are you have a Gerry Barber story. While most have been embellished over the years, Gerry has confirmed a few. Like the time he and two waiters took on a gang of twenty Satan's Choice toughs. Gerry claims he ended the fight when he knocked out their leader and the rest quit. Like the time he went toe-to-toe with Canadian boxing champ Yvon Durelle, who had narrowly lost to heavyweight champ Floyd Patterson. Gerry called that one "a draw."

He admitted to beating the heck out of several Ottawa Rough Riders over the years, and assorted baddies armed with crowbars and baseball bats, and even had a Molotov cocktail thrown through his living room window. He couldn't get life insurance because no company would take the chance. Tough job, tougher guy.

But as scary as Gerry Barber could be when he took off his glasses and balled up his fists, most musicians loved the guy. It was Gerry who would protect them from the drunks and rowdies. Rick Lemieux of The Eyes of Dawn says, "Gerry Barber was always nice to us, and I think he took a shine to me because I was so young. He was always telling me to stay out of trouble."

THEE DEUCES/THE HEART

For a band that "couldn't play very well," with a frontman who was "a pretty bad singer," The Heart did pretty well for themselves in the mid-'60s.

The roots of the band go back to Almonte, Ontario, when they were called Thee Deuces and specialized in instrumental rock. But seeing as this was 1964, the focus soon turned to the new wave of music from England. "We covered a lot of British bands, like the Animals, some Beatles tunes and a fair amount of Rolling Stones songs because they were simple," remembers John Martin, AKA the "pretty bad singer."

John's first band was the legendary Barons with Bob Coulthart. On nights off, he loved to hang out at the Midtown Ballroom and later the Oak Door to check out the cool bands coming in from out of town, the resident Hi-Tones and other local acts. One band he liked was Thee Deuces, and when he was approached to join the Almonte band he jumped at the opportunity.

What he lacked in vocal prowess, John made up for with his natural flair as "an entertainer." "We did some James Brown material, with the band doing horn sounds, and I got to drop down on my knees and stuff like that. It's probably the most fun I've ever had."

A forty-seven-week residency across the bridge at the Inter-Provincial Hotel in Hull was key to making Thee Deuces a tighter unit. After that came a non-stop run of church and school dances, and those amazing package shows at the Coliseum, Auditorium and Hull Arena that featured up to ten local bands with non-stop music and sellout crowds.

John Martin remembers one show vividly, just after they changed names from Thee Deuces to the more contemporary "The Heart." "I can remember playing at the Coliseum and we pretty much started a riot. At the Hull Arena Dave [guitarist Dave Liberty] got torn off stage, and when he reappeared, he was in his underwear and shoes. The girls had torn his clothes off. That was funny. The same thing happened in Ottawa. It was like a kind of mania that was going through the fans at the time."

Thee Deuces, the pride of Almonte

A record deal and two releases on Sir John A Records followed, taking The Heart up a step in the pantheon of local rock bands. The name change idea actually came from Richie Patterson from The Esquires, who took an interest in helping the band. John Martin thought that Richie had tired somewhat of his role as a drummer in The Esquires by 1966, and was looking for something different, which perhaps included getting into band management.

But it turned out to be a lost opportunity for The Heart that still irks John. "To this day, I think if we hadn't been so stupid and so full of our ourselves, Ricky would have made us a hit, because he knew everybody. He thought we had potential. We didn't have the talent, but we were entertaining. He was just full of great ideas, like the stickers we used to give out at shows. It was like someone was handing us the golden ticket and we were saying no thanks, we don't need this."

The famous sticker

And for a while it looked like The Heart didn't need any help. Their booking schedule was full, thanks in large part to Lennie Alexander, who booked the group in some pretty wild spots. John's favourite story is about the night The Heart travelled to Smiths Falls for a gig. "We played one night at an arena in Smiths Falls. We were the opening act for a wrestling match featuring André the Giant. Back then it was cheap to hire a band, and all you needed was an elevated platform and a plug. We got into big trouble when we played a gig in Almonte at the Town Hall. The stage was slanted so we had to put nails in the stage to keep the drums from sliding off the front of the stage. They didn't like that!"

It was all fun times for The Heart, until they lost a member and headed off to Toronto to find a replacement. They came back with a guitarist and, according to John, a new problem. "We found a new guy named Junior. He suited the band well. But he brought a guy named Peter Jermyn with him who had been the organ player with Luke and the Apostles and was looking for a new start in a new city. We sort of inherited him. Man, he was way above us. I think after three or four months he was bored with us and wanted to do something else. Around this time, Bobby Coulthart and Doug Orr left The Esquires, and they were looking for something to do. So,

Peter and I met at a restaurant at Sparks and Bank and the four us walked out as members of a new band called The MRQ."

As for The Heart, they soldiered on with new addition Marc Corbin, but after one more single for RCA in 1968, the band folded.

The legacy of Thee Deuces/The Heart is simple…they were entertaining. There were no epic guitar solos or intricate harmonies to impress other musicians. They were a true band for the people, there to have fun, play their hearts out, put on a show, hand out some stickers and move on to the next gig. As John told me, "You owe it all to the people who come and see you. They are the ones who make your life worthwhile at the time. You don't have an audience, you don't have a damn thing."

SOME "IDOL CHATTER" WITH HARVEY GLATT

Maybe you've never met Harvey Glatt, or even heard his name, but chances are you've walked past him at a concert, or stepped into his record store, enjoyed an artist he has mentored, or listened to his radio station. In short, Harvey has been a towering figure on the Ottawa music scene since he helped bring folk legend Pete Seeger to town in 1957.

That experience connected the young entrepreneur/music fan to promoters in Toronto and Montreal, and set the stage, literally, for an eclectic music circuit that ran between the three cities.

In September 1957, Harvey opened Ottawa's first standalone record store, Treble Clef Records on Slater Street. Later, under the Bass Clef moniker, he started booking legendary acts like Bob Dylan, The Rolling Stones, The Beach Boys, Cream, The Who, Jim Hendrix, Led Zeppelin and all the other acts you remember fondly from your wild youth.

The radio station came in 1977, when CHEZ 106 burst onto the airwaves with an eclectic mix of current hits and new artists. It was an important part of your musical education if you grew up in this area in the '70s and '80s.

But probably his proudest achievement was his partnership with Dennis Faulkner in a cozy little club that started on Bank Street then moved to Sussex Drive called Le Hibou.

I asked Harvey what the vision was for the club.

> **HG:** *I look at it as coming together of visual artists, musicians, and actors. It was a synthesis of things happening where they all influenced each other. Sometimes the music was very folky and traditional, and other times there was jazz. We had Weather Report come in for example. A lot of it was rock-oriented or folk rock. My partner Dennis Faulkner booked the French artists from Quebec.*

The "music pipeline" Harvey had created with Toronto and Montreal resulted in many extraordinary nights at Le Hibou, some of which are listed later on. It became a great hang-out for Ottawa musicians, who soaked in music from artists they had never heard of before, and styles that were miles away from the pop fare being played on the radio. It was, as Dick Cooper of the Cooper Brothers says, "an education for all of us."

Before September 1957, there were no real record stores in Ottawa. There were several places to buy records, but most of them were in department stores like Frieman's or Zellers. Harvey changed that with his first Treble Clef store. One of his earliest customers stood out, in more ways than one.

> **HG:** *Our first store was very briefly on Slater Street. This big, heavyset guy would come in quite often. In those days we had listening booths, and this big guy would be bouncing around to the records he was listening to. We got to know*

> *him, and he certainly knew about music. About a year later he got hired to work at our store on Rideau Street.*

The "big guy" was Brian Murphy, better known as "The Source" to radio listeners on CFRA, CKBY and, most famously, on CHEZ in the years to come. Brian was, like Harvey, a music educator, exposing us to jazz, blues, folk and rock of all styles through the medium of radio. He and Harvey shared a deep personal bond till Brian passed away in 2005.

Harvey has a similar relationship with a young singer/songwriter named Bruce Cockburn.

> **HG:** *I first heard his music at Le Hibou. I never thought he was the greatest singer in the world, but I was very impressed with his creativity, and I thought the guy was extremely intelligent. I used to take him to see some European films to expose him to different things. I managed him as a solo artist for a while. I remember he was doing a gig one time in Toronto and most people walked out, but the people who really knew were impressed. Very often, when someone is so original, it is hard for people to accept something that is too far from what they are used to. It often takes a while to acquire a taste for good things. I remember going to hear folk festival auditions at a club in Toronto. There was a young woman who got up and sang, not necessarily in tune, but her name was Jane Siberry. I was really impressed with her because she was different, special, and there was a talent there. Later on she did pretty well, and never to everyone's taste. We booked her later on at Le Hibou.*

Siberry was also heavily promoted by CHEZ-FM, which was an enormous boost to her early career.

After a stint as manager for The Esquires, Harvey turned his attention and efforts to a band of Le Hibou regulars who called themselves The Children. I asked him about that experience.

> **HG:** *I didn't put them together. They just kind of evolved out of the Le Hibou scene. The principal influence was Bill*

Hawkins and his music. Bill was very important in helping Bruce Cockburn learn to write songs. It didn't last very long. Sandy Crawley was probably the best singer in the group. They had a bit of a following. I had them open for a concert in Toronto at Maple Leaf Gardens with the Lovin' Spoonful and The Association. Somehow Bill was sitting there playing, thinking "I don't want to be part of this."

JH: What brought you out so often to see live music?

HG: Curiosity is the word. A lot of the time I got out and it was a disappointment. In more recent years, people would ask if I could go out and hear them, and when I would show up before they played I'd say I have another obligation so I might not be able to stay for the whole set. But if I really liked it, I would say I'd liked it so much I gave up on the other event. That was my escape valve.

JH: How should you be remembered?

HG: I think of myself as a catalyst. The whole motivation for selling music, records, and putting on concerts is to share with people and introduce different musical artists to people. Curiosity is a big part of my life. People ask me why I would do this or go there. It's because I'm curious.

GEORGE HARRISON VISITS OTTAWA (?)

No book on the Ottawa music scene of the '60s is complete without a mention of Le Hibou Coffee House, which spent much of that decade in its "classic" location on Sussex.

I won't attempt to go into the various phases and owners Le Hibou went through, or the incredible artists who played there or just dropped by, but some are mentioned in this book.

The definitive book on Hibou is Ken Rockburn's brilliant *We Are as The Times Are – The Story of Le Café Hibou*. You can get it through https://burnstownpublishing.com.

But there is one story I want to touch on, and that concerns the night a Beatle came to town.

Although attempts were made to bring the British pop sensations to Ottawa on their first tour, we had to settle for two solo visits. John and Yoko visited the capital in 1969 and had their famous meeting with Prime Minister Pierre Trudeau. And in 1968, George Harrison made a surprise visit to Le Hibou Coffee House to check out a performance by folk singer Eric Andersen, who was being considered as an addition to The Beatles' Apple Music roster. It is chronicled on Le Hibou tribute pages, Beatles fan sites and local papers. There are numerous, well-respected eyewitnesses to his presence, and maybe someday someone well erect a plaque to commemorate that momentous date—February 28, 1968. Too bad it's not true. For the first time, here is the real story behind the legend of George Harrison at Le Hibou.

The story seems plausible enough. In 1968, The Beatles launched their Apple Records label. It was to be the home for future Beatle albums, solo projects and any other artists that the band "discovered." Those artists would include James Taylor, Mary Hopkin, Badfinger and Ravi Shankar. The idea was to stay small and very exclusive. With the band itself starting to fray at the edges, it was also a nice diversion for John, Paul, George and Ringo.

According to legend, George Harrison came to Ottawa in late February with two other Apple execs on a scouting mission to check out an American folk singer named Eric Andersen who was playing to Le Hibou. Andersen came out of the famed Greenwich folk scene, and quickly rose in the folk ranks thanks to his strong song-writing abilities. Beatles manager Brian Epstein was a huge fan and was in the process of signing a management deal with Andersen when Epstein died in August 1967. It's safe to say George was also a fan—otherwise why would he freeze his ass off in Ottawa, Canada in late February to see Andersen play?

But it turns out George wasn't freezing his butt off that night in Ottawa. Instead he was basking in the hot sun of northern India, learning all about transcendental meditation from Maharishi Mahesh Yogi with the rest of The Beatles. He was there from February 15 to April 13, 1968. To make the picture even muddier, Eric Andersen was not booked to play Le Hibou on the night of February 28, 1968. So that makes the legendary visit an impossibility.

Time to hit the Google machine. One account had George in Ottawa on that date to see Andersen, and adds that during the day he also went to the Capitol Movie Theatre to see *Yellow Submarine*! Now that movie came out in July 1967, and I doubt it would still be on screens six months later.

So, I searched "Eric Andersen in Ottawa" to check out his play dates. There was one from February 28, but in 1969, not '68. Okay, fair enough. Someone got the wrong year for the encounter. But on that night Eric was playing at the Capitol Theatre on Bank Street. Wikipedia told me George indeed came to town February 28, 1969, to check out Eric at the Capitol and then went off to Le Hibou to watch the after-hours show with Ottawa's MRQ. Okay, there it is. Some details were lost in the haze of time, but that's what happened.

Then I got an email from Eric Andersen. I had flipped him a note asking if he remembered that fateful night. Well, Eric remembers playing Le Hibou several times, but, to his knowledge, he never played the Capitol Theatre and he had never met George Harrison. My head started to hurt, but I plowed back onto the Google machine. This was getting interesting.

This from Dave Brown's "Below the Hill" column in the *Ottawa Journal* from March 4, 1969: Rumours flew earlier this week to the effect that George Harrison, one of The Beatles, visited Ottawa and made a stop at one of the local coffee houses. One newspaper carried a report on the visit by quoting a few persons who said they saw him. This made me curious. Was he really? We put this question to Arma Andon of Apple Records, who is also The Beatles' U.S. Business Manager, by phoning him in New York. He said he visited Ottawa that week himself, but was the only 'Apple' producer in town. As for Harrison: 'Not a chance,' said Andon."

Could it have been an imposter "George" who pulled a prank to get into Le Hibou for free? Everybody looked like a Beatle to some extent in 1968, or '69, or whatever.

So, Apple Records denied he was here. Eric Andersen says he never met George. The dates and venues are mixed up. And what's with this mysterious Capitol Theatre connection? Is there nothing to connect Eric Andersen to The Beatles?

One more Google. How about "Eric Andersen / Beatles / Capitol Theatre"? WTF!!!

If this were *Storage Wars*, this would be the part when someone opens that old suitcase in the back of the storage locker and says, "What the...?" and then they break for commercial. No commercials in books, so let us proceed.

This was the "Holy Grail" moment in my search for George: an ad from the February 14, 1969, edition of the *Ottawa Journal*. It promotes a show at the Capitol Theatre on February 28, 1969. It reads "Take A Trip With the Beatles, In Magical Mystery Tour. Plus, Eric Anderson on Stage." They got the spelling wrong on "Andersen," but that is pretty common. There were two shows for this odd pairing, with tickets starting at $1.50! This looks like there were two showings of The Beatles' British TV special *Magical Mystery Tour* with Eric Andersen playing between showings.

TAKE A TRIP WITH THE
BEATLES
In Magical Mystery Tour
Plus
ERIC ANDERSON ON STAGE
1 NIGHT ONLY CAPITOL THEATRE
FRIDAY, FEBRUARY 28 — 7 P.M. and 9.30 P.M.
TICKETS
$1.50 - $2 - $2.50 - $3 - $3.50 - $4
Available at both Treble Clef Record Stores
177 SPARKS STREET   68 RIDEAU STREET

Ottawa Journal, February 14, 1969

It was all true! Eric Andersen was in Ottawa that night, and there was a Beatles connection. There were potentially two reasons for George Harrison to be in town that day. First, to see the film, and second, to, perhaps, see Eric play live. There is no documentation to prove the latter, and Eric never met George, but a late-night trip to Le Hibou to catch some music afterwards makes sense. And we have those credible eyewitnesses!

Our conclusions, after this long day on the Google machine, are that George Harrison was in Ottawa on February 28, *1969*. Eric Andersen did play a show at the Capitol Theatre that same night. George Harrison was most likely in the Theatre and saw Eric. Whether that was his prime reason for being there is unknown. After that show George and his small entourage either walked or were driven down to Le Hibou, where they saw The MRQ play their after-hours show. They then walked the two blocks back to the Château Laurier for some sleep, likely freezing their asses off.

So, there we have the real story of George Harrison's visit to Ottawa. The legend re-lives!

THE CHILDREN AND THE MRQ

The traditional way of starting a band was beginning to be challenged by the second half of the '60s. The common method of starting a group was to get some high school buddies together, make some noise in the garage and then start scoping out teen dances. Along the way, natural selection kicks in and the weaker members either quit and get real jobs or are replaced.

But as musicians and bands got better, the talent field improved while shrinking in size. This separated the kids who were in it for the chicks and fun and those who in it for the chicks and a profession. Players like Gary Comeau, John Bacho, Doug Orr and Ted Gerow could virtually pick what band they wanted to be in, changing loyalties when opportunities arose. The international music scene was not much different, as we witnessed the age of the supergroup!

Cream was first in 1966, when Eric Clapton (Yardbirds), Jack Bruce and Ginger Baker (John Mayall's Bluesbreakers), the "cream" of the British blues scene, combined forces for the *Fresh Cream* album. When they broke up in 1968, Clapton and Bruce teamed up with Steve Winwood (Traffic) and Ric Grech (Family) for a one album project called *Blind Faith*. *Super Session* featured super-session guitarists Mike Bloomfield and Al Kooper, and Steve Stills from Buffalo Springfield. Then came Crosby (Byrds), Stills and Nash (Hollies). Neil Young (Buffalo Springfield) joined a bit later.

While all these projects resulted in classic albums, the lack of interpersonal chemistry doomed them to failure, and the concept faded out quickly.

Here in Ottawa we had two supergroups, one of which fizzled out pretty quickly and one that made the jump from the '60s the '70s before folding. The first was called The Children.

The Children

He can't remember precisely how it was arranged, but on April 24, 1965, folk singer Sandy Crawley and his buddy Neville Wells were standing in the wings at the Ottawa Auditorium waiting to open for The Rolling Stones. "Neville, Bob Langeau and I worked up a three-song set which, I think, included 'King of the Road' by Roger Miller. I don't even know if we had a name," Sandy told me. "We shared a dressing room with The Rolling Stones because it was their first time in North America. We were sitting in a hockey rink dressing room with them. Nobody heard a word they were singing because of the screaming. The girls just wanted to see Brian Jones."

At the time Sandy and his musical friends turned up their noses at Rock and Roll. They worshipped at the feet of Bob Dylan, Ramblin' Jack Elliott, Lightnin' Hopkins, Hank Williams and Ray Charles, and were regulars at Le Hibou Coffee House. The friends included Sandy, Peter Hodgson (alias Sneezy Waters), Neville Wells, David Wiffen, and poet-songwriter Bill Hawkins.

Although Hawkins was the least musically inclined member of this loose fraternity, he was the key to getting the group off the ground. His poetry had garnered the attention of Harvey Glatt, and that support was golden.

According to Sandy Crawley, Harvey came up with the money to buy the equipment they needed to get started and even offered them a practice space in one of his Treble Clef stores. Two of The Children also worked at Bass Clef selling guitars.

The first official lineup for The Children in late 1965 was Neville Wells, Peter Hodgson (later known as Sneezy Waters), Sandy Crawley, Chris Anderson and Bruce Cockburn. It was a dazzling array of talent, with Bill Hawkins as an unofficial member handling song-writing chores with Bruce. Cockburn had learned his chops a the Berklee School of Music, where he majored in composition and arranging. One of Bill's tunes was "It's a Dirty Shame," which became a sizable hit for The Esquires. Hawkins also served as band manager.

One newspaper article described The Children as "The Epitome of Cool!" and while the group had all the potential in the world and the right sound for those days of folk rock, the band never really got off the ground. There were some great gigs, like the opening slots for the Lovin' Spoonful and The Beach Boys, but there were no records, no radio play, no big TV appearances and no real recognition outside of Ottawa, and even that was minimal despite the unique material and talents involved. They did have a fan club they called "The Children's Revolutionary Army" that cost fifty cents to join, and it attracted a solid, hard-core group of fans. But overall, The Children were spinning their wheels after nearly two years together, so it came as no surprise when Peter and Chris stepped out. Their replacements had great credentials, as would be expected in The Children. Richard Patterson took the open spot on drums, and David Wiffen took Peter's position.

In 1968, Sandy left, but before he did, he offered some sage advice to Bruce. He told Bruce, "You've got to be solo. You're too strong." Cockburn hung in for another four or five months and then he was off to Toronto to find fame as a solo artist. It's clear he can look back now on those days and appreciate the opportunity he had as a writer and arranger in The Children.

So, if it wasn't lack of talent or original material, why did The Children not succeed? Sandy Crawley has some thoughts on that. "We gave it a good shot. We went down to Toronto and recorded a demo. But we were just young kids. We had ego and tension stuff. I think that we could have made it. Neville was our leader in the sense that he was the oldest member and the most responsible, straight-up stand-up guy. I was pretty undisciplined, and Sneezy (Peter) was the wild man. He always will be. I think we lacked that fire in the belly that could have taken us to another level."

The Toronto demos formed the nucleus of a "Greatest Hits" collection on True North records released in 2013. The depth and breadth of the material is staggering and amplifies the cries of "What if?"

In 1997, with much fanfare, Bruce Cockburn, David Wiffen, Bill Hawkins, Richard Patterson, Neville Wells, Peter Hodgson and Sandy Crawley reunited for the first time in thirty years for a well-received set at the Ottawa Folk Festival. Cockburn made no secret of the fact that his time with The Children helped shape his career in the music business and his subsequent success.

David Wiffen said this to reporter Rick Overall of the *Ottawa Sun* before the show: "I think what stays with me most about The Children was the group's originality. I had never come across so many songwriters all in one city. It was a breath of fresh air for me when I found them."

DEDICATED FOLLOWERS OF FASHION

"Clothes make the man."
Quote attributed to Mark Twain

But, do clothes make the band?

Brian Epstein seemed to think so, and you can't question his judgement.

In their Hamburg days, The Beatles favoured black leather and a tough image on stage. Epstein changed that, when he put The Beatles in matching suit ensembles to present them as a professional, tight unit, suitable for prime-time British TV.

The Stones, on the other hand, were encouraged by manager Andrew Loog Oldham, to adopt a more casual, on-the-street look, and it to worked in their favour. It set them apart from The Beatles and helped cement them as the anti-Beatles, the street kids who were true rock and roll rebels.

The clothes helped create identities for both bands, even before they played a note.

Like every other scene on the continent, Ottawa was split pretty well in half when it came to band garb. Bands like The Esquires, The Townsmen and particularly The Staccatos favoured the clean-cut suit-and-tie look of The Beatles. Others, like Don Norman and the Other Four, The Skaliwags and The Scoundrelz went for the edgier look of the Stones, with casual clothes and grim scowls in the publicity posters. What you saw is generally what you got.

The Mojos

The End Dees

The Townsmen had their outfits tailor-made at Le Château on Rideau Street. Later in the '60s, the coolest hippy fashions could be found in the market at Lovey and Clives. But for matching Carnaby Street duds or casual street fashion, the place to shop for hip clothes in the '60s was Chuck Delfino's on Bank Street.

Chuck made a lot of money dressing Ottawa bands because of his business savvy. At least once a month, Chuck would fly down to New York City to check out the latest hot fashions for trendy kids coming over from "Swinging London."

Frank Morrison of The Townsmen was a regular customer. "Chuck would buy the clothes in New York right off the plane from England and bring them to Ottawa." he recalls. When a new shipment of paisley or big-collared shirts came in, the line would be out the door as musicians battled to stay on top of the local fashion pile.

Chuck's son Gordie Delfino played in The Scoundrelz, so Dad also created some of the outrageous stage outfits worn by the band.

The very fashionable Eastern Passage

Some bands took it a step further, using their wardrobe to tell a tale of some historical significance. Gary Puckett and the Union Gap wore American Civil War outfits, while Paul Revere and The Raiders were Revolutionary War characters. The Count Five, of "Psychotic Reaction" fame, wore capes and played vampire in their early years.

In this area, we had The Boston Tea Party, who appear to have raided Old Fort Henry for their uniforms. They were part of Don Billows Progressive Group Management talent roster.

The Boston Tea Party

PERSONAL MANAGEMENT
HARVEY GLATT
c/o THE TREBLE CLEF LTD.
177 SPARKS ST.
OTTAWA 4, CANADA

The Modern Rock Quartet, MRQ for short, took their shot in 1968, and while they didn't reach the rock stratosphere, they were probably Ottawa's most interesting and creative band of the latter years of the decade.

Like The Children, The MRQ was the right band for the times. These were the early days of the progressive rock movement, with British bands like King Crimson, Pink Floyd and The Nice turning out amazingly daring albums, mixing rock with jazz, classical and psychedelic influences. Like The Children, The MRQ had plenty of talent and a unique sound, but never quite got the breaks that could have made them international stars. But when it came to musical prowess, no Ottawa band could match The MRQ.

The MRQ story begins in Toronto in the late '60s. In a music scene that boasted a number of highly respected rock and R&B bands, Luke and the Apostles stood out as being very, very different. They started as an electric blues act in the mid-'60s, then evolved more into a driving rock band that sounded like a cross between Mandala and the Ugly Ducklings, two of Toronto's hottest acts.

Luke and the Apostles attracted attention from American heavyweights Bill Graham, Albert Grossman and Paul Rothchild of Elektra Records, who would soon discover an L.A. band called The Doors. The band signed with Elektra, released one single and did an acclaimed two-week stand at the legendary Café Au Go Go in New York City.

With expectations soaring, the group went home to Toronto to decide their future, and shortly thereafter broke up when lead singer Luke Gibson jumped ship to join the Kensington Market, another Toronto band with an album and a bright future. Keyboard player Peter Jermyn moved to Ottawa where he played briefly with The Heart, then hooked up with Heart singer John Martin and Doug Orr and Bobby Coulthart from The Esquires in the summer of 1968. Thus began the strange saga of The MRQ.

The MRQ Mach 1: Martin, Jermyn, Coulthart and Orr

Interest in four stellar players with recording experience was high in the record business, and soon they had signed a deal with RCA Records. The one single from that relationship was "Plastic Street" in 1968, which failed to crack the pop charts but still sounds really good, even fifty years later.

Having no guitar player, The MRQ was driven by keyboards and a rock-solid rhythm section, and Martin's vocal were strong enough to fill in any holes. The music was an intriguing mix of rock, jazz and classical, with Jermyn writing the bulk of the music. They also did their own unique takes on several tunes written by Bruce Cockburn, who had been briefly in The Esquires with Orr and Coulthart. The most commercial they got was a cover of Cream's "Sunshine of Your Love." If you went to see The MR, it meant you were in for a very interesting evening of music.

But the eclectic, progressive approach of The MRQ also created problems. No matter how critically acclaimed the band was, they had trouble getting bookings. The MRQ was also part of Leonard Alexander's stable of bands. "I loved what they band was doing musically because I was a musician myself," says Lennie. "The problem was that they just weren't right for most of the venues I booked because they weren't a dance band, and they didn't play any familiar songs. And that is what kids at high school dances and sock hops were looking for."

Playing with Jermyn in The Heart had been challenging enough for John Martin, but trying to figure out what he was doing in The MRQ was even tougher. "I was really thrilled to be with these guys, and that's where I learned a lot about singing, because Peter just played what he played, he really wasn't accompanying you. So you had to be an instrument. Sometimes we were just shooting way above the heads of the audience. We always missed a guitar, but Peter didn't want anything else there to cloud his image."

John Martin was replaced by Brian Lewicki, back with his old mates Bobby and Doug. It was not an easy transition for either Peter or Brian. "They would do an opening jam that might go twenty minutes and then the song would start. They were so many time changes and so many mood swings," Brian remembers. "I had to practice with them every night for about a month and a half before we could do a short set at Le Hibou. I think I was brought in partially because I had lots of experience in the studio and I had the power in my voice."

Brian also brought his legendary drive for success to the band, which went contrary to Peter's vision for The MRQ. The word "compromise" was not in his vocabulary, and that had to frustrating for Brian, Doug and Bobby. The volatile chemistry project that was The MRQ was starting to boil over.

By this time, The MRQ was spending as much time in Toronto as they were in Ottawa, although they remained regulars in the late-night slot at Le Hibou for years. That was the perfect venue for the group, in front of an audience that granted exploratory artists the freedom and respect to be themselves. They backed up major acts like The Who, Janis Joplin, The Grateful Dead and Procol Harum at a memorable stand at the Electric Circus in Toronto. Peter, especially, was more comfortable in that kind of setting than playing in bars. And that is a major reason why he decided to leave the band after a trip to Japan for a gig at Expo '70.

Brian says the very nature of The MRQ's material put them in a tough position to move forward as a recording act: "One recording exec said, 'There are three or four really good singles in this one long piece.' But Peter didn't want to cut it apart and compromise. We could only play in specific places because we weren't a dance band, we were a concert band. That's what we were about."

So, as he did with The Esquires, Brian pushed for change in the music and the way the band operated. That meant hitting the club circuit and making the music a bit more accessible. Peter didn't like it, and he was gone.

The MRQ spent a few more years playing the circuit at Le Hibou and at clubs up and down the Ottawa River till they died a natural death – once again, leaving a lot of promise behind them.

Peter Jermyn returned to Toronto, where he still performs his music his way.

FINAL THOUGHTS

I was twelve years old when Beatlemania hit Ottawa. Being a shy youngster, I never fully partook of the '60s social scene. My first concert was Wilson Pickett at the Capitol Theatre, and I did manage to see Cream there in 1968 thanks to my dad, who had read about them in *Time* magazine and bought tickets for me, my sister and my brother. In short, I was not one of those young kids who lined up to see The Esquires at Pineland or the latest hot bands at Parkdale United Church. But boy, did I love the music!

I was that other breed of fan who lay awake under the covers late at night listening to my "Rocket Radio" with the antennae in the nose. My school grades were bad enough, thanks to Gord Atkinson's *Campus Club* and Nelson Davis during study hours. But it was when radio signals miraculously appeared out of the night sky from exotic places like New York City and Buffalo that things go really magical. The fast-talking American DJs made our boys sound almost sleepy—that is, till Al "Pussycat" Pascal arrived on the local scene with his non-stop platter chatter and cool characters.

Al's *Final Hour* was my favourite radio show, with the long, hippy album tracks, and bands I had never heard before, like The Chambers Brothers, Chicago and the long versions of hit songs by The Doors. I never knew "Light My Fire" was such a great song till I heard the album version.

We watched Ed Sullivan and the Hollywood Palace every week and saw our heroes. That's where I fell in love with the Vanilla Fudge, The Young Rascals and The Who.

My most vivid musical moment came in 1964 when I was riding my bicycle near our home at 129 Fourth Avenue in the Glebe near the corner of Lyon, and this blast of music from a balcony almost blew me off my bike. It was the drum intro to "Bits and Pieces" by The Dave Clark Five.

I rode around in circles till it was over. That summer I got the "Bits and Pieces" album for my birthday. It still hangs on my wall, right beside my autographed photo of Dave Clark.

My perspective of the Ottawa music scene in the '60s was different than most of the people I had the honour of talking with over the course of writing this book. I was a spectator, and they were the participants. So when I decided to do a kind of "bridge" chapter to explore the impact the '60s scene in Ottawa had on the bands that did well in the '70s, I knew I had to talk to someone much, much older and experienced than me. It had to be Dick Cooper.

Now just in case you spent the '70s outside the country, The Cooper Brothers were the second Ottawa band to gain attention outside of Canada—the Five Man Electrical Band, of course, being the first.

After some local and regional success with a few singles produced by Les Emmerson, the Coopers made a huge career leap in 1978 when they signed with Capricorn Records, the home of the Allman Brothers, the Marshall Tucker Band and other southern rock superstars. They did two albums with Capricorn, toured with legends like the Doobie Brothers, Joe Cocker and others. Their biggest song, "The Dream Never Dies," remains a staple on classic rock and adult FM radio.

Dick and his brother Brian have been there and has done that!

A FINAL "IDOL CHATTER" WITH DICK COOPER

JH: When did you start playing in bands?

DC: I might have got a bit of a late start when it came to getting into bands because, first of all, I wanted to get a degree to fall back on. I only went full time into music in the early '70s, although I played a bit with my brother Brian in the '60s. But I was totally aware and influenced by the local scene. Vern Craig was married to my cousin, and because of that I knew about The Staccatos, and Les and I became good friends and later bandmates, and we still are! Terry King was a member of The Eyes of Dawn, and he eventually became part of our band, Emmerson, Cooper and King. I would go out to see bands on dates and I would see the 5D, The Esquires and all those guys. There were so many church dances too. I remember when I was really young going to see David Clayton-Thomas, before he was in Blood, Sweat and Tears, and his band The Shays at our neighbourhood church. I was too young to get in so I kind of peeked into the window and I thought, 'Wow. That's a real band.' And once you got over a certain age, there was Hull, and you were going to see the Playdates at the Glenlea, and then up and down the Aylmer road strip. And you could catch the travelling bands at the Ottawa House. It was amazing how much there was to see in one night.

JH: Was it only rock and roll for you at the time?

DC: Oh no, I really got into going to Le Hibou and exposing myself to other music. I was a rocker, but then I would go to Hibou and go, 'Oh wow. Blues is cool. Jazz is cool. Folk is cool too.' I think that really broadened my horizons. Le Hibou was such a cool place to go and hear different kinds of music. It kind of helped your musical education along a bit too. I think I would have been a completely different kind of writer if I hadn't been into the Hibou scene.

JH: How would you compare the Ottawa scene with the Toronto music scene in the '60s?

DC: In Toronto, there was a huge R&B influence for the local bands. And I think here in Ottawa it was strictly British Invasion and kind of Beach Boys stuff. And that's why we had so many bands in Ottawa with great harmonies. There was a real clear demarcation between the two scenes. With the Cooper Brothers, we always had the harmonies, but what made us different was that we had a bit of the country thing going. Bands like The Hollies were a huge influence on the Ottawa bands.

JH: It must have been a wonderful time for a music lover to grow up in Ottawa.

DC: Any night you could go out and see a band. Nobody was bingeing on Netflix or playing video games. I can just remember thinking, well where are we going to go tonight? There were just so many clubs, dances and bands. All those bands got played on the radio, and that sure doesn't happen now. Back then, before all the stations were owned by one or two companies, you could have a regional hit. That happened to us before the Capricorn deal. A station down east started playing our record and we went down there and toured for a couple of weeks, made some money, then came home. Nowadays you hear the same records on all the stations, so you don't get that.

JH: What local bands were your favourites?

DC: I loved The Staccatos and The Esquires, and Terry King's band The Eyes of Dawn. And I really liked a band called The Characters. I especially liked and admired the bands that did original material.

The Characters

JH: It must have been inspiring to young musicians coming up to see an Ottawa band have a #1 hit like "Signs."

DC: Exactly. Even before the Five Man hit, I would go see them and think that here is a band from Ottawa that is getting radio play and recording records, so why can't we do this? I remember sitting at a table with David Wiffen and Bill Hawkins of The Children a while back, and I told them how much of an influence they had on young musicians back in the '60s. I told them that they inspired us to keep going and trying different things. I'm glad I got the chance to tell Bill that, because he died shortly after. Those guys were heroes to me. It gave me and my brother the belief that a couple of kids from Bell Street can do this too.

BITS & PIECES

We can thank geography for a great deal of the live music we enjoyed in the '60s and '70s. Being on the road between Toronto and Montreal, Ottawa was an easy stopover for the major acts who began touring Canada in the mid-'60s. Without the 416, I doubt we would have got acts like Elvis, Cream, Hendrix, Led Zeppelin and The Who. And without a visionary like Harvey Glatt, would we have seen Neil Young, Joni Mitchell and Gord Lightfoot in a coffee house? Doubtful.

Here are some great concert events from Elvis onwards at some of our best venues. Give yourself 2 points for every concert on this list you saw. If you still have the ticket stub, that's good for 3 points. Good luck!

THE AUDITORIUM

APRIL 3, 1957: Elvis Presley for two shows. Top ticket price: $3.50

NOVEMBER 18, 1957: "Show of Stars 1957," featuring Ottawa's own Paul Anka, Fats Domino, Frankie Lymon, LaVern Baker, The Everly Brothers, The Crickets, Chuck Berry, Eddie Cochran, The Drifters, Buddy Knox. The top ticket price for all this legendary talent was $3.50. On stage, Paul got a Golden Platter Award for over one million sales of his first hit "Diana."

NOVEMBER 3, 1964: "The Big British Bash," with Gerry and the Pacemakers, Billy J. Kramer and the Dakotas and The Staccatos. This was the first visit to town by British Invasion acts.

FEB. 20, 1965: The Beach Boys, Big Town Boys and The Staccatos

APRIL 24, 1965: The Rolling Stones, The Esquires and J.B. and the Playboys. Top ticket: $3

JUNE 1, 1965: Herman's Hermits, Bobby Vee, Little Anthony, Freddie Cannon and others

SEPTEMBER 4, 1965: The Beach Boys and The Esquires

FEBRUARY 19, 1966: Bob Dylan. According to the review in the *Ottawa Citizen*, "On stage he moved from one wailing lament to another without benefit of a master of ceremonies or self-introduction. If perception was difficult during the solo stint, it was nigh impossible during the second stint with the big sound of the Hawks from Toronto as a backdrop. It is this kind of deviation and the resulting 'folk rock' sound that has sparked unkind criticism from folk-song purists, who consider this innovation the worst kind of heresy."

APRIL 30, 1966: Gene Pitney, Len Barry, Chad and Jeremy, The Outsiders, Bobby Goldsboro

JUNE 18, 1966: Twelve-hour show and dance with The Esquires, The Skaliwags, The Barons, The Children, Thee Deuces, The Townsmen, The Eyes of Dawn, Don Norman and the Other Four, Thee Group, and other local acts

THE COLISEUM

FEBRUARY 1, 1958/JUNE 18, 1960: Johnny Cash

FEBRUARY 19, 1964: Roy Orbison

MAY 16, 1964: Bobby Curtola and The Staccatos

JUNE 18, 1966: Bruce Cockburn

DECEMBER 28, 1966: The Young Rascals, The Paupers, Thee Deuces and The Jesters

> **THE YOUNG RASCALS' DANCE**
>
> featuring **THE YOUNG RASCALS**
>
> FROM TORONTO PLUS
> **THE PAUPERS THE DEUCES**
> **THE JESTERS**
> **OTTAWA COLISIEUM**
> LANDSDOWNE PARK
> **WEDNESDAY DEC.28**
> 8:00pm
> Special Limited Advanced TICKETS $2:00
>
> Available at
> THE TREBLE CLEF STORES
> 177 SPARKS STREET
> 68 RIDEAU STREET
>
> Regular Admission—$2.50

MARCH 1, 1967: The Animals, The Eyes of Dawn and The Townsmen

CAPITOL THEATRE

MARCH 28, 1966: Petula Clark

NOVEMBER 24, 1967: Roy Orbison, Colleen Peterson, St. Patrick's Street Rooming House and The Eyes of Dawn

JANUARY 28, 1968: Wilson Pickett, 5D, Colleen Peterson and The Flying Circus

FEBRUARY 5, 1968: Simon and Garfunkel

MARCH 15, 1968: The Hollies. After the show, Graham Nash of The Hollies went down to Le Hibou Coffee House to see Joni Mitchell. They started their celebrated relationship that night.

MARCH 19, 1968: The Jimi Hendrix Experience and The Soft Machine for two shows. The first show started with a cover of The Beatles' *Sgt. Pepper's Lonely Hearts Club Band*. After the late show, Jimi went down to Le Hibou to catch Joni Mitchell. He sat by the stage and recorded it on his tape machine. The show was labelled "a bomb" by *Ottawa Citizen* writer Bill Fox: *"In two Capitol Theatre shows Tuesday, The Jimi Hendrix Experience failed to live up to its advance billing. His stage presentation is unorthodox and unpredictable. Often his comments are lost. Most of the time the noise from the instruments drowned out the voices."*

SET LIST FOR JIMI HENDRIX EXPERIENCE LATE SHOW
- Killing Floor
- Tax Free
- Fire
- Red House
- Foxy Lady
- Hey Joe
- Spanish Castle Magic
- Purple Haze
- Wild Thing

APRIL 8, 1968: Cream. After the show, Eric, Jack and Ginger decided that it was time to break up the band. After fulfilling their remaining concert obligations, they played a "final" show at the Royal Albert Hall.

```
— CREAM —
IN OTTAWA MONDAY, APRIL 8 AT THE
CAPITOL THEATRE.
ON TUESDAY
GO TO YOUR FAVOURITE RECORD STORE
FOR

— DISRAELI GEARS —
JUST ONE OF TWO LP'S BY
THE CREAM
ON POLYDOR
```

OCTOBER 30, 1968: Gary Puckett and the Union Gap and The McCoys

MARCH 20, 1969: Tommy James and Shondells and The 1910 Fruitgum Company

APRIL 15, 1969: Joni Mitchell

MAY 21, 1969: The Who performed "Tommy."

LE HIBOU (Just scratching the surface)

LE HIBOU
521 sussex dr.

JANUARY, 1969: Neil Young:

JUNE, 1965: Gordon Lightfoot:

JUNE, 1967: Joni Mitchell:

JULY, 1964: **Bruce Cockburn** first played with Sandy Crawley

October 1968: Tim Hardin:

March 1963: Ian and Sylvia:

January 1968: Muddy Waters:

August 1968: Howlin' Wolf:

February 1963: John Lee Hooker:

October 1969: Van Morrison:

October 1969: Doc Watson:

HERE AND THERE

```
OPENING NIGHT
THE ESTABLISHMENT
SATURDAY, JULY 15th
FEATURING
THE 5D
8:30 – 11:30         $1.00 PER PERSON
```

FEBRUARY 9, 1963: Del Shannon at the Oak Door

SEPTEMBER 30, 1965: The Sparrow, later known as Steppenwolf, with The Hi-Tones at the Oak Door

JUNE 3, 1966: The Haunted (Montreal) at the Strand Hall, Bank and Riverside

The Haunted is here!

JUNE 3, THE GROOVE (Strand Hall, Bank St.)
JUNE 4, PINEGROOVE (Pineland, Riverside Dr.)
JUNE 5, THE PLACE (Glenwood Bowl, Aylmer)

HEAR 1,2,5 – LIVE

$1.00 Per Person   Dress – Casual

JULY 1, 1966: The Ugly Ducklings (Toronto) at the Strand Hall

MARCH 10, 1967: The Stampeders at the Ottawa House in Hull

MARCH 16, 1968: The Guess Who from Winnipeg played Ottawa for the first time at the Canterbury Community Centre. A week later, they were at The Barn in Aylmer.

AUGUST 23-31, 1968: "Where It's At Youth Pavilion" at the Ottawa Ex. Mandala (Toronto), Lew Kirton Soul Revue, The Townsmen, The Marshmallow Soup Group, MRQ and The Eastern Passage.

NEWSLETTER

THE EASTERN PASSAGE

The **Eastern Passage** are Canada's hottest new act. Their latest release "I Could Make You Fall In Love" f/s "Feel So Fine" on the Zoo label is doing extremely well on both sides of the border. See **The Eastern Passage** at the "EX" where its at show Wed. Aug. 28.
For Bookings Contact
DONALD BILLOWS, Promotion House, 233-4509
East West Agency, 236-5830

JANUARY 28-FEBRUARY 2, 1969: Neil Young at Le Hibou.

AUGUST 15, 1969: The Mothers of Invention at the new National Arts Centre.

SEPTEMBER 10, 1969: Chicago Transit Authority, before they were forced to change their name to just "Chicago," at the National Arts Centre.

OTTAWA CIVIC CENTRE

FIRST CIVIC CENTRE ROCK SHOW: JULY 16, 1968

Tickets for this show at Treble Clef started at $1.50. Ottawa's 5D opened the night, followed by the bubblegum band The Ohio Express, Britain's great pre-punk garage band The Troggs, and headliner The Who.

The review from the *Ottawa Citizen* read: "*The Who finished the show by hurling guitars in the air, smashing mics and stands, throwing amps and bashing drums across the stage. It was a wild, wooly and expensive finish. The crowd loved it.*"

JANUARY 17, 1970: Steppenwolf

MARCH 23, 1970: Five Man Electrical Band

APRIL 14, 1970: Led Zeppelin

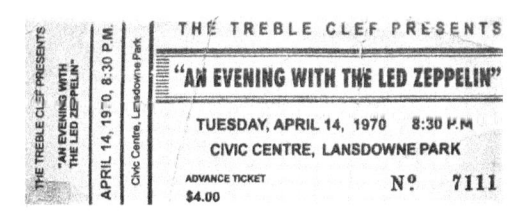

MARCH 15, 1971: Grand Funk Railroad

JULY 19, 1971: Black Sabbath, Yes and Alice Cooper

TONIGHT
8 p.m.
TREBLE CLEF
PRESENTS

BLACK SABBATH
Warner Bros. Recording Artists
WITH SPECIAL GUEST STARS

ALICE COOPER
AND BRITISH MUSIC SENSATION

YES
OTTAWA CIVIC CENTRE

TICKETS $5.00

Tickets at all three
Treble Clef Stores.
Tickets $5.00

JUNE 3, 1972: Jethro Tull

APRIL 19, 1974: Genesis, *Selling England by the Pound* tour

JUNE 15, 1974: David Bowie, the *Diamond Dogs* tour

DECEMBER 10, 1974: Rush

MARCH 15, 1975: Stevie Wonder

SEPTEMBER 7, 1975: Peter Frampton

APRIL 22, 1976: Kiss, *Destroyer* tour.

JANUARY 27, 1977: Queen, *A Day at The Races* tour.

JANUARY 29, 1977: Styx on the *Crystal Ball* tour

APRIL 22, 1978: Meatloaf, *Bat Out of Hell* tour. Near the end of his energetic show, Meatloaf fell off the stage and broke his leg.

MAY 2, 1978: David Bowie, *Low* and *Heroes* world tour

OCTOBER 14, 1978: Peter Gabriel. This was his first solo tour after leaving Genesis.

NOVEMBER 3, 1979: Bob Marley

JULY 16, 1980: Van Halen

JULY 20, 1981: Tom Petty

ODDS AND SODS

NOVEMBER 31, 1977: The Vibrators at Oliver's Pub, Carleton University. This was the first punk rock show in Ottawa.

DECEMBER 20, 1975: Bruce Springsteen and the E Street Band, National Arts Centre

MARCH 10, 1981: U2, Barrymores

> Chaudiere Club, Aylmer—Mankind (Rose Room), Silent Sorrow (Green Door), today, Sunday at 9 p.m.
> Barrymore's, 323 Bank St.—Mitch Ryder of the Detroit Wheels, today, 9 p.m. March 10, U 2 from Ireland; March 12-14, Rhinegold.
> La Hutte Restaurant, 36 St. Louis, Pte. Gatineau—Patrick Norman, guitarist, Tues. to Sat., 9

APRIL 9, 1975: Supertramp, Chris De Burgh, Ottawa Technical High School as part of the *Crime of the Century* tour

AUGUST 5, 1978: The Eagles, Rideau Carleton Raceway

DECEMBER 5, 1981: Iggy Pop, Carleton University Gym. This was the same night as Genesis at the Civic Centre.

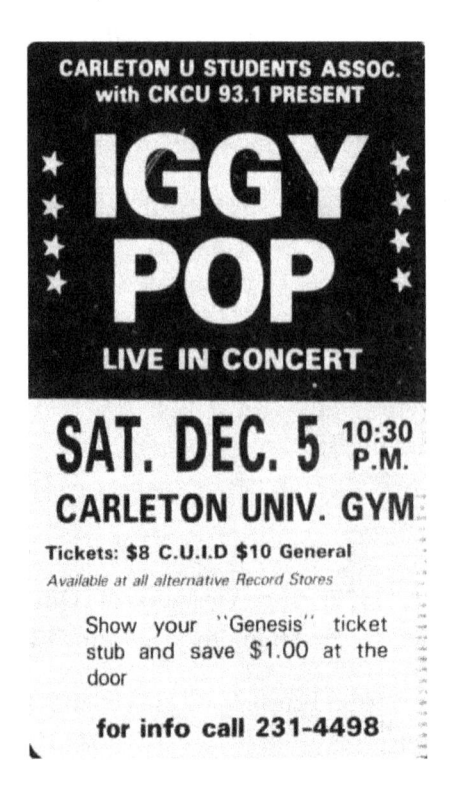

> **CARLETON U STUDENTS ASSOC.**
> **with CKCU 93.1 PRESENT**
>
> ★ **IGGY** ★
> ★ **POP** ★
>
> **LIVE IN CONCERT**
>
> **SAT. DEC. 5** 10:30 P.M.
>
> **CARLETON UNIV. GYM**
>
> Tickets: $8 C.U.I.D $10 General
> *Available at all alternative Record Stores*
>
> Show your "Genesis" ticket stub and save $1.00 at the door
>
> **for info call 231-4498**

TOP FIVE OTTAWA SINGLES OF THE 1960S (?)

It's always fun to make your own "hit parade" or playlist for your iPod. These are, in my opinion, the best five Ottawa singles put out in the 1960s in the pre-"Signs" era.

Half Past Midnight (1967 Capitol)...The Staccatos

Juno Award winner, the first Ottawa rock single to feature strings, immaculate recording and harmonies. This is a hands-down #1 song anywhere in the world!

Heartbreak Hotel (1966 Red Leaf)...The Scoundrelz

Covering an Elvis hit takes guts on its own, but re-shaping and re-modelling such a familiar song earns big bonus points.

The Lion Sleeps Tonight/We're Doing Fine (1966 Regency)...The Townsmen

This was the perfect song for the harmony-rich Townsmen. It's another case of a great local song that should have been a cross-Canada hit.

The Bounce/All of My Life (1966 MGM)…Don Norman and the Other Four
What strings did for "Half Past Midnight," a rockin' horn section did for "The Bounce." It's an infectious combination of the "Let's Go" beat and the Dave Clark Five sound that make this tune "bounce" off the radio speakers.

Baby Boy (1967 Sir John A.)…The 5D
Brad Campbell of the 5D calls their first single "The perfect summer, blast-out-of-the-radio kind of tune." Can't argue with that.

LEST WE FORGET

The majority of bands covered in this book had the good fortune of being immortalized on vinyl. Others, unfortunately, are remembered only through fuzzy promo pictures or word of mouth. There is no way to ensure every band is represented in *Rockin' on the Rideau*, but we've tried to be as inclusive and comprehensive as possible.

Thanks to super-researcher Ken Creighton, here is a list of the bands who never made it into the recording studio, but who deserve our respect and thanks for their music.

For those who rocked, we salute you!

THE BANDS

Barons (The)

Bathtub Ring

Beaux Gestes (The)

Bitter Sweet (The)

Blues Image

Book (The)

Boston Tea Party

Brass Bull (The)

Carousels

Censored

Children (The)

Dedicated Love (A)

Doormen (The)

Elastic Band

Eton Show Band

Everlovin'

Exhibit A

Grains of Sand

Grape

Group Called Bubs (A)

Illuminated Picture (The)

Insects (The)

Jesters (The)

Knicknacks (The)

Larry Sweet Blues Band (The)

Lemon Creek Bridge

Lew Kirton Soul Review (featuring Ottawa guitar great Roddy Elias)

Mood of Blue (The)

Missing Links

Mojos (The) – see The Bittersweet

Morning Glory (The)

Music Machine (The) (featuring brothers Pat and Stevie Travers)

Musical Fantasy (A)

National Gas

Nirvana

Outcast (The)

Pop Art Pillow

Prophets (The)

Purple Haze

Raphaels (The)

Reactions (The)

Reasons Why (The)

Renaissance

St. Patrick Street Rooming House

Sheltered Souls (The)

Shelves of Darkness (The)

Society (The)

Sons of Adam & Eve (The)

Sticks & Stones (The)

Stone Age (The)

Sunday Connection

Telstars (The)

Thee Group

Treble Tones

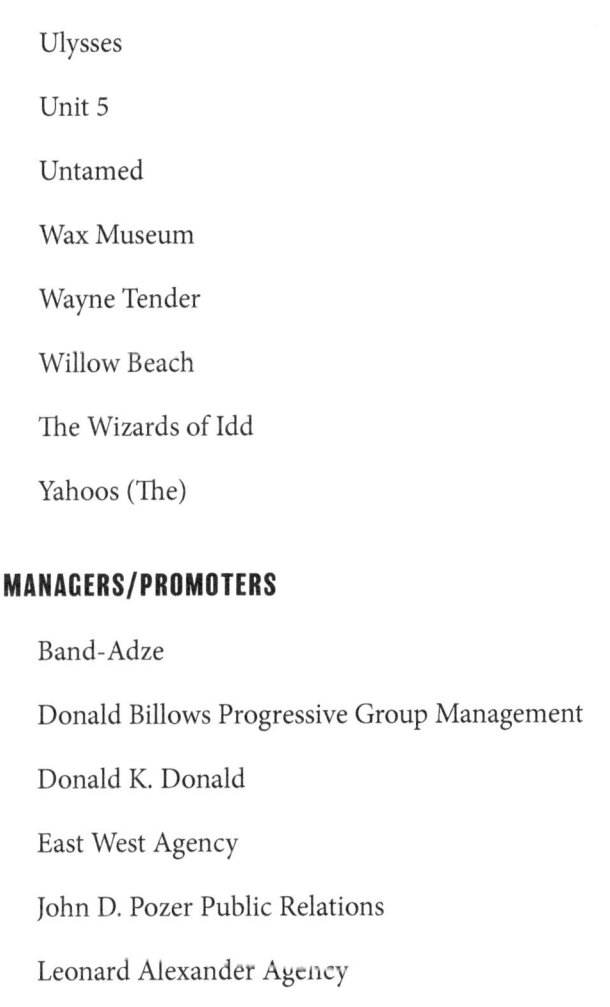

Trippers (The)

Tyme & A Half

Ulysses

Unit 5

Untamed

Wax Museum

Wayne Tender

Willow Beach

The Wizards of Idd

Yahoos (The)

MANAGERS/PROMOTERS

Band-Adze

Donald Billows Progressive Group Management

Donald K. Donald

East West Agency

John D. Pozer Public Relations

Leonard Alexander Agency

> Representing Canada's Top Entertainments
> **leonard alexander agency**
> 116 O'CONNOR STREET,
> OTTAWA 4, ONTARIO
>
> BOOKING — Dances — Shows
> Concerts Tours
>
> Big 12 Show booked Exclusively by
> leonard alexander agency
>
> For Information Call — Ottawa (613) 235-0578
> 235-3712
> Monteal (514) 695-9284
>
> Serving Canada's Music Industry

McConnell & Associates

The Swing Set Agency

> **OTTAWA'S NEWEST BOOKING AGENCY**
> The Swing Set AGENCY
> CONTACT: — DOUG McKEEN
> 236-9603 or 235-6830

Triangle Productions

Vern Craig Enterprises

Thanks to all these people for the great memories and greater music. And thanks for reading this book. I hope you enjoyed it.

Jim Hurcomb

September 11, 2020

ABOUT JIM HURCOMB

Unless your mom hid your transistor radio in 1973 and still hasn't given it back, chances are you know who Jim Hurcomb is.

From 1973 to 1980 Jim was one of the most popular voices on CKCU-FM, Radio Carleton, Ottawa's first cool FM station. From 1980 – 2000 he hosted a number of programs on CHEZ-106, including the afternoon variety show *In The city*, the very loud *Power Chords* and the flagship *Morning Show*, first as half of *Geoff (Winter) and Jim*, and later *Jim and J.R.* (John Rogers). Then it was 8 years at CFRA co-hosting *Middle Aged, Bald Guys* with Al Fleming. These days, some 47 years after pushing that first button, Hurcomb is still behind the microphone, hosting and producing *The Sound of the Underground* on LIVE88.5, heard Sunday nights at 9.

Away from radio, Jim is deeply involved in other aspects of music, as a musician, teacher, music trivia host and writer. *Rockin' on the Rideau* is his first book. If you like this one, there may be a *Rockin' On The Rideau: The 70's* late in 2021.